BAN

THIS

BOOK

The ongoing spread of fascism in the USA

by

CHRIS S. BUCKLEY

WORKBOOK PRESS LLC
187 E Warm Springs Rd,
Suite B285 Las Vegas NV 89119 USA

Website: https://workbookpress.com/
Hotline: 1-888-818-4856
Email: admin@workbookpress.com

Ordering Information:

Quantity sales. Special discounts are available on quantity purchases by corporations, associations, and others. For details, contact the publisher at the address above.

Library of Congress Control Number:

ISBN-13:   978-1-961845-33-6 Paperback Version
                978-1-961845-09-1 Digital Version

REV. DATE: 02/09/2024

For Diana

INTRODUCTION

J ust as every good story has a beginning, a middle and an end, so too do all forms of trouble have three parts. It has a cause, an effect and it has solutions. We'll be dealing with all three. Because what good does it do to discuss *cause* and *effect* without dealing with *solutions*? It'd just become another rant, and who needs another rant? I sure don't. It might bore me even more than it might bore you, the reader, though onward we trudge.

On the subject of cliches, I'd be remiss not to mention "You can't see the forest for the trees." Here, we'll look at a whole host of nifty procedures with which to find our way *out* of those pesky trees, so that we might take in more of the forest.

Do you believe "America First" was a phrase thought up by our forty fifth president? Far from it. Do you think fascism has only been around a few years? Think again. You'll see quite a few references to politics and politicians throughout, because it's politics and the Supreme Court that make the laws by which we, as lifetime members of Planet Earth, pursue our happiness.

So, let's discuss that *pursuit of happiness*. The phrase, or a facsimile of same, can be found in every item, from the American Constitution, to a movie line, to, yes, a line in a book. And not without good reason. Everything that we, as human beings, do, from the moment we draw our celebrated first breath, is confined to within that same pursuit. Animals? No different. It is a happiness that is fleeting at best, but usually well worth the wait. We play as children, grow up and fall in love, maybe start a career, get married, work at jobs that most of us don't like, and perhaps have more children, all because we honestly believe these things will make us happy.

Some make themselves happy by taking away the above mentioned merriments, quite abruptly, in less than five seconds, with a bomb or maybe a gun. Let's be clear, guns do kill people. Any nonsense about people killing people does not apply. If the gun hadn't been manufactured in the first place, neither would there be the temptation, or in some cases, the urgency to use it. Guns and bombs are manufactured solely for the purpose of *killing*, and nothing else. Even cops are trained to shoot to kill.

Contained in my first book, "Man Of A Thousand Jobs" (now out of print) is a detailed account of my having witnessed the one and only human being I've ever seen shot dead by another. Most people go through entire lifetimes without ever seeing what I saw, but lucky me, I happened to be in the wrong place, at the wrong time, and found myself with more life experience to pass along. Though I haven't figured out how, or in which chapter, I intend to reprise the shooting experience here, perhaps word for word. The reason? Judging by book sales and a total absence of royalties, I figured out that not very many people have read that first book. At last count, it was two. And the story, teeming with all its gory details, needs retelling to all who can listen to, or read it.

Regarding past publications, my second book, "Call Out The Dolphins," which, by the way, didn't exactly fly off the shelves, but did do better in sales than the first, closely compares each and every human lifetime to the Solar System in which our lives take place, and how we're all responsible for what goes on in our individual Solar Systems. Some might call it 'driving our own bus.' Bus or spaceship, it really doesn't matter, so long as you are in command of said vehicle. In the pages that follow, we'll re-examine the same concept, while on a more organic level. Exciting? Not very. But most informative. Then maybe we'll discuss *doing or saying the right thing*, while in control of the bus.

What the reader will also see is a description of books that are banned in most of these United States, and, usually, the reasons; s/he'll see a comparison of school days of the 1950s and early 60s, with school days of the present, replete with active shooter drills; as a reader, s/he'll see a breakdown of the human lifetime, to age eighty and beyond, and why your guide considers it a miracle. All of this shrouded in subtle, though at times, not so subtle fascism, here in these United States of America.

Here, we'll ask simple questions, and answer them with what will almost certainly be simpler answers. Because, when all else fails, what is it we do? We *simplify*. We'll find answers steeped only in *logic* and common sense. That's why I, a person of average intelligence and education, am so willing and able to answer the questions. "Why hasn't this been done before?" you may ask. It has, though in different ways, to which readers may have paid close attention while reading, but to which no one paid much attention, in the pursuance of their daily lives. How do I know this? Because nothing's changed.

There'll be no mention of race, race relations or critical race theory; no mention of gay people – well, maybe one – or how to describe them; no mention of the 'Durham Report'; no mention of transgender bathrooms, except that, like unwanted pregnancies, creating bans or laws that forbid them will *not* make them magically go away. What there will also be are descriptions of fascism, disguised as democratic politics as usual, and of course, solutions.

On the subject of miracles, we'll examine, as mentioned, the human anatomy, hence the more "organic" level. Hopefully, it'll give readers more of an appreciation for same, and less of an inclination to abruptly take it away from someone. I claim no medical degree or high IQ. I'm average at best. But, for the second time, what is written by me is based on *facts*, with a generous sprinkling of editorial commentary, and nothing more.

Somewhere, we'll have to discuss gullibility. This subject is where I start to get a little short on patience. In 1978, the self-proclaimed Reverend Jim Jones was able, with not much effort, to convince a little over 900 directionless people, that drinking Kool-Aid, spiked with generous amount of potassium cyanide, would help them all, on their journey to the promised land. He was right. After obediently gulping down the deadly concoction, they all died. Unknown whether or not any of them reached the bliss promised by the Reverend. My guess would be that they found nothing more than the mud in which they perished. More about Jim Jones later.

As a child, and throughout my teenage years, I, personally, was known for my own gullibility. "Make up anything, he'll buy it." True enough. I'd buy it. While I shan't go into any long-winded examples, suffice it to say, you could tell me anything, and I'd probably believe it. But then, during my adult life, I encountered certain followers of multiple fascist cults, and I have to say, here and now, they've got me beat. I've legitimately met my match.

At a youthful age, I had a teacher who imparted some wisdom to all of us seven and eight year-olds, that has stayed with me throughout the decades. Her name was Miss Smith. Yes, so far as this seven year old knew, that was her real name. On the first day of school, she announced, after having taken the roll and snapping her attendance book shut, "Everyone starts out with an "A". What happens to that "A" from this day on, is entirely up to you." She continued to talk to the class, as though we were adults. "You can keep it an A, or you can let it fall to a B, C, D or an F. It's up to you. Right now, there's a whole column of A's in this book, and it's up to the students whose names are next to those A's, what happens next." I like that policy. So much, that I made it my own, for the duration of this lifetime. From third grade to the present and beyond, everyone starts with an A.

Authors of early science fiction, including the original 'Star Trek' TV series, seemed to hold out great hope for the American future. Stories that take place in a future where it's presumed that world peace has taken place; people of all colors, religions and political persuasions have collectively kissed and made up; they've all laid down their guns and other weapons of mass destruction, in favor of world peace; and they've redirected all that energy, negative or otherwise, to the mystery of the stars. But those authors neglected to consider one thing, without which our utopian future simply can not exist. It's present, though not prevalent, in every society. It requires, but seldom gets medical attention, and in some cases, medication. It's called *mental health*. Why does this author bring up such a sensitive subject, here and now? Mental instability comes in all sizes, shapes and ages. It's even possessed of some world leaders. With regard to sizes, shapes and ages, there are many more than I, your humble author, am medically qualified to impart. I know enough, however, to know that were it not for peoples' mental health or lack thereof, or their inability to grow into rational adults, attempts at gun control might not be an issue in my native land.

Now let's discuss fascism. It is what we're here for, no? A very fine line exists between fascism and democracy. So fine, that it's often nonexistent. It's been said that fascism never dies. Logically, it never does. It merely uses another form, usually human, to continue promoting itself, advancing itself, in one way or another, onward, toward the destruction of whatever happens to lie in its path. Ruination and cruelty are all it knows. Building things – except bombs and guns – is beyond fascism's comprehension. It knows only how to destroy. A beautiful building or cathedral that may have taken hundreds of years and, as was the case in Northern California, millions of slaves, to assemble, can be destroyed in seconds, with a single bomb. A human lifetime, for which birth announcements were once sent, after having drawn its first breath, and a lifetime that evolved into man or womanhood, can be abruptly ended with a single, well placed bullet. In either of the above cases, fascism has successfully done its work.

Fascism works 24/7. It takes no off days or holidays. It's ever-present. And the glory of fascism is that *you*, from politician to everyday supporter, *you*, from ship's captain to bellhop, *you*, the burgeoning fascist, will never have to consciously seek out fascism. It'll find you soon enough. It'll overwhelm you. It'll make you believe you're doing the right thing. Hurting people? Killing people? Not a problem. Why? Because all the while, fascism or the concept of fascism will have you believing that you're doing a *good thing*, for the good of the human race.

Fascism has many tools, through which it works to commit its sinister deeds. There's greed, power, politics, religion, unchecked mental health, and the most powerful tool in its box, hate. Now and again, people walk around believing they're full of *hate*, when, in actuality, they're not. As a fine line exists between democracy and fascism, so too does a fine line exist between love, hate and tolerance. Take, for instance, the 1/6/21 overrunning of my homeland's Capitol. Media proclaimed, in practically every other sentence, that the "rioters" were so full of hate. Truth be known, they were not only happy, they were having the time of their lives. It's the hate, you see, that made them happy. The hate, the destruction, the terrorizing of other human lives. All of it made them, the terrorists, feel gleefully happy. Not to mention, superior. They're a part of something. Never mind that the 'something' was originally spawned by hate.

Each of us has a destiny for good or for evil. Much as I would like to take credit for the preceding line of clever dialogue, I can not. It was first spoken in "Casablanca," arguably the greatest love story ever filmed. The line makes only one point: **From softball games to world wars, you'll have to pick a side**. Right or wrong, it's the way the human race has evolved. For all that is good, there's an evil side that waits patiently, or sometimes not so patiently, to destroy it. Why? Because without evil, there'd be no need for good.

It's not my intention to tell you, the reader, what to do, how to live your life. If, however, you can benefit from my life experiences and the *facts* herein, then by all means, take what you will and leave the rest. I hail from a generation that once claimed it would eventually change the world. This is a part of my contribution. And it won't be easy. How could I have known there'd be a whole new batch of pasty faced fascists, spawned usually by the uneducated, and waiting in the wings, to pick up where Richard Nixon left off, and in the process, make him look like a Boy Scout? Naivete, mostly. Perhaps I should've known that fascism has been smoldering in my homeland since the 1930s, awaiting just the right moment or moments to rear its misshapen head. And be assured, it will. Feel free to set your watch. Fascism and its related concepts have nothing but time.

1.

To start small is the way of all successful endeavors. My native land started with only thirteen states, then better known as colonies. Things start small or simple, then eventually, with a little soldiering, they become complicated giants. Guns are no exception. The very first gun brought to our shores, before we were even a viable country, was brought by Columbus, and was called the Arquebus. It was a single shot, front loading, long rifle. Over the next 300 years or so, the firearm didn't show much progress, mechanically or aesthetically. In my homeland, meanwhile, James Madison would propose the storied "Second Amendment" in 1791, which has long since become a political tool, used mostly by self-styled conservatives. They hide behind the Amendment, shortly following present day mass shootings, when banning assault weapons is the logical course of action.

About a hundred years later, in 1891, the NRA (National Rifle Association) was established by William Conant Church and George Wingate. It has since become a monstrous non-profit organization, with a current available revenue of $412.2M, according to Britannica. Meanwhile, back in 1791, Madison's proposal, during a period when the American population, according to the census of 1790, (the first ever census), was 3,929,214, would be accompanied by the only two guns procurable in 1791. There was available to the paltry public, the musket and the flintlock pistol. The musket had a one-round magazine, and, in the hands of an experienced shooter, could fire about three rounds per minute. I'm curious to know if our readers believe that, had there been AR-15's or Uzis, or any other 900 round-perminute weapon of war in existence during ratification of the Second Amendment, would the Founding Fathers have followed through with their signatures? Me thinks not.

On June 26, 1934, the Congress of my homeland passed the NFA (National Firearms Act), while concurrently outlawing the machine gun, a definite weapon of war, but also a weapon with which local police forces could not compete. The new law, which still stands, was intended to curtail "gangland crimes of that era, such as the St. Valentines Day Massacre." If that particular American mass shooting is not known to you, the reader, your host humbly suggests that you google it.

The inventors of, and ultimately those who benefit monetarily from the sale of every AR-15 have said, sometimes publicly, that the weapon was never intended for private ownership. From where I sit, I don't see any of those beneficiaries falling all over themselves to support federal legislation, financially or otherwise, that would prohibit private ownership of this particular weapon of war. I could be wrong. I hope I am.

Another hesitant member of the start-small-get-bigger family would have to be the intentional destruction of libraries. Libraries, you see, are informative outlets, where people can rely on edifying books. They are a place or places where everything from fictitious classic novels to memoirs to how-to guides can be found. Books based on *facts*, gathered by authors, who wouldn't dare to write them, without first gathering said facts. This, coupled with a free press, can not be tolerated by despots.

Our own Library of Congress was among the first buildings to be destroyed during the War of 1812. They started small. In the next century, however, during World War II, libraries, one after another, across Europe were surgically destroyed, when Hitler had visions of becoming their (fascist) dictator. The 1998 film "Pleasantville" depicts young people, lining up to get into the town library, after finding out there is actually something written on the pages of books. In her 1980 address at the Library of Congress in my homeland, Barbara Tuchman said "Without books, the development of civilization would have been impossible." I couldn't agree more.

Moving right along in the realm of our subject at hand, we can also find the human lifetime. It surely starts small, microscopic I dare say, then grows. And grows. And grows. The lifetime starts innocently enough, as an embryo. It is then that we are all the same size. The very first thing we all touch, while in the womb, is, interestingly, our genitals. A sort of introduction to masturbation? Not much else to do, tho, huh? Okay, so then we draw that celebrated first breath – the breath I referenced in pages past – and out of our mouths comes the first sound we make, a primal scream. What follows is an encapsulation of the human lifetime, which is unimpeded by bullets or bombs.

Ages 1 – 8. This is the age group that forms our personality for the rest of our life, be it long, to the extent of 110 years, or , through circumstances over which we have no control, mostly because of our age, short. So short, we don't make it to nine. It's the age range during which our front teeth fall out, and are replaced by the permanents. Each of us will face at least one life threatening situation before we die. Some of those situations, depending on our age, will actually take our lives away, in the wink of an eye. People in this age range, however, know little or nothing about the concept of death. Without education, they grow up to be adults with little or no concept of death. The closest thing they've seen are video game characters, or cartoon characters, who magically return to life with each quarter, regardless of how much blood they've shed. The human being is the only mammal on the planet that knows, after a certain age, that it's going to die.

In my second book, I tried to emphasized that the number one job of a small child is to *have fun*; that Christmas, Halloween, birthdays and County Fairs are expressly for this age group. I don't think I was very successful. It (having fun) is, after all, the one thing we do best, mostly because we haven't had time to learn much else. Bill pay? Love? Heartbreak? Violence? Those are all adult issues, supposedly. For now, let's have some *fun*. Everything's fun. If it isn't fun, we'll figure out how to make it fun. Let's pretend! You can be the cowboy and I'll be the spaceman! Together, we'll find a way to defeat the eighteen foot tall monster, and make the world safe! On the topic of eighteen foot tall monsters, a word to parents: Unless you're playing with the kids, try not to *be* that monster. The small child turns to one of the only two adults it knows personally, for comfort, shelter and reassurance. Do you give the child all these things, or is it easier just to be the monster?

Somewhere, during the first eight years of our lives, we'll experience the third grade. I bring it up because the third grade is where your humble host learned all or most of what he uses to this day. Addition, subtraction, telling time, reading, signing my name, cursive, etc. There's a book entitled "All I Really Need To Know I learned In Kindergarten," by Robert Fulghum. Must have been an accelerated program. I had to wait until the third grade.

Ages 9 – 20. I personally can assure you, the reader, that there are a few of these years upon which I've looked back and asked myself, sometimes aloud, "What the hell was I thinking?" But then, if you're not rebelling, in some way, even if that way is horrifically stupid, put simply, you probably should think about getting out more. You now have, and can enjoy the *freedom of choice*. To an extent, you had it as a child, but usually made the wrong choice. I implore you to use it wisely, this time around.

At some stage of this segment, usually the early teens, you'll have all the answers. Who knows how or why, but you'll have an answer, usually wrong, for everything. And disdain for anyone, typically parents, who don't. It will matter not to you whether you're right or wrong, only that you have the answer. Should siblings be involved, your job will be to hate them, almost as much as you hate your parents. This is also the point at which some will run away, some will take their own lives, but most will simply suck it up, roll their eyes and acquiesce. I believe it was Einstein who said, [para] "Such a pity that youth should be wasted on the young."

Some may become athletic, and maybe even go on to the pro's. Football, baseball, basketball, tennis or swimming. Regardless of the sport, always remember that only you can determine how far you go, and at this age, the sky's the limit. Speaking of famous quotes, it was Arthur Godfrey who once asserted, among other things, that to become perfect at anything, you must practice that thing for no more than fifteen minutes a day. After having tried this theory many times, I can assure you that a few more minutes a day probably wouldn't hurt.

It's usually during the high school years that, hopefully, someone – maybe an instructor? – will introduce you to the concept of balance. Should that happen, please pay attention. To keep all things in their proper perspective is a large part of becoming a rational adult. This juncture will determine whether your allegiance to, say, football is an obsession or is kept in its proper perspective; or perhaps whether you're able to ask, calmly, and in normal vocal tones, why a weapon of war is being sold, not only to civilians, but to eighteen year old civilians. The concept of gun-toting children has no place in the fields of logic or common sense. If there's no balance in your life, however, you're probably on the trigger end of that weapon of war, anxiously awaiting the opportunity to use it.

But I digress. These are the real wonder years; the ages at which you're going to live forever, and death is always something that happens to other people, routinely on the 6 O'clock news. Senility is for the aged. The aged that we'll never be, because – have you heard? – we're going to live forever.

For some, these years might include the military, around which your lives will revolve for two years, four years, or perhaps a lifetime. Regardless, you're now willing to be trained at your chosen profession.

Remember how you wished, with all your heart, when younger, for these adult years to finally arrive? Well, here they are. Now, what are you to do with them? These years are transitory. One day, sooner than you believe, you'll awaken to find the impending time of your retirement, and wonder "Where did all those years go? They were here a minute ago." Ah, but you were too busy, living life, to notice how quickly the decades pass. And now here you are, getting ready for your retirement party. Some may wait, well beyond the legal age of withdrawal from the workforce, believing that 'retirement means death,' or some may have jobs from which you just don't retire, such as, but not limited to attorney, journalist or actor.

Generations come (of age) and they go. They do the work that needs doing, then, little by little, each generation dies off. Every generation leaves something for the next to deal with. The WWII generation left, for my generation, nuclear weapons. We, in turn, left the AIDS epidemic for the next generation. There are people in their twenties and thirties, who've never known a life without the threat of AIDS. Regardless of what the generation that precedes yours happens to leave, you can be sure of one thing, it'll take many lives, before it saves lives by the millions.

It was once declared by author Ken Kesey that each decade is not ten, but thirteen years in length. Makes sense. A good example would be the decade of the 1960s. All of the 50s fads, music and patriotism remained until 1963. Pick any decade from the 20th to the 21st century. You'll find that it didn't really last ten years. More like thirteen.

Ages 21 - 40 If there are careers to be had, money or mistakes to be made, love to fall into and out of, property to be acquired or babies to be born, these are generally the ages between which they can all happen.

Ages 41 – 60. There's an old belief that 'life begins at forty'. They always leave off, or maybe just omit the second part of the proverb, 'and ends at fifty'. Me thinks that second part was written or recited by someone who didn't have much luck in his or her fiftieth year. Year fifty, if we so desire, is a great time for a career change. We still have most of our brain thrust, and our bodies – well, for most of us, the body will follow. A career change can be exciting. The world is still your oyster. Year fifty, however, can also be a time of great anxiety. The family arguments or alcohol or both may have taken their toll, or perhaps age has become an issue. This could be where the career change comes in. I, personally, started film school at age fifty five.

We'll begin with hair color. Get that grey out. You won't lie about your age, if asked, but you'll definitely not speak unless spoken to. Then comes the body. The one that refused to follow. A small matter of the pot belly, typically on men. Then there's night school. In later chapters, we'll discuss the ease at which one can enter a college or university. Choose something that intrigues you, so you won't fall asleep during the lectures. Sometimes the most intriguing of subject matter, nonetheless, can not compete with a lack of sleep. I speak from practical knowledge. Now, you're ready to begin your brand new career. And only fifteen or so years till retirement.

Our fifties can also be the age range wherein the 'bill' comes due and payable for all those edible frivolities enjoyed during our teens, twenties, thirties and forties – fast food, candy, ice cream, alcohol to excess, et al – all consumed when grave illnesses only happened to other people, like our parents. But we paid it no mind, because it simply can't happen here. Late Onset Diabetes is common among this age range. Whether it's Cancer, Diabetes, Leukemia or something else minor that could become major, we'll march off to the doctor, and follow his or her instructions to the letter. We'll take our medications religiously, and if physical therapy is involved, we'll never be late for an appointment. Why? Because most of us have the instinct to survive. An instinct that was placed at birth and evolved, along with our pursuit of happiness.

Ages 61 – 80. Having come of age in the home of my grandparents, I know a little about the unfairness of the aging process. I graduated high school and watched both of them retire, she from clerking, he from the electrical trade. All their friends were around their age or older. Then I watched them get older. I never paid much mind to their witticisms or wise proverbs, which could only have been learned from their life experience, except when I got my first car, a '57 Plymouth. Bought from Dad, who, in passing, once said, "Ya know, the first three letters in the word funeral...spell fun." That stuck. Maybe it was his delivery. She died first, at age 93. About ten years later, he followed, at 89. In keeping with our theme, things will continue to go from small to big.

When entering our septuagenarian years, exploits such as a simple trip downtown, which, at one time in our lives, was an effortless annoyance, will now become a very big deal. And the older we get, the bigger the deal. Long car trips, which were once something to look forward to, now become dreaded and fraught with worry. Most of us are 'homebodies' now. Nothing to be ashamed of. Lots to do at home. Laundry, dinner, breakfast, lunch, and all the dirty dishes and clothes that go with them. What's the hurry? Let's take our time. These are our 'golden years,' where we can walk from one room to the other, stand in the middle of said room, wonder why we made that trek, and all without fear of ever being judged. Heard about a gentleman who, for the heck of it, drove the entire distance, from Albuquerque to Los Angeles, in the right lane, with his left turn signal on.

It's during these decades that we'll have put together our "bucket list," and will now make it a point to do everything on the list, constipation notwithstanding. This is also the age range during which there are sometimes a few things to do, but always things to forget to do. Perhaps a comfortable chair would be in order, strategically placed in the room into which we walk. The chair is so we can sit down and be comfortable, while we search the memory banks for the reason we entered the room.

We'll begin to believe that life is passing us by, when the reality is that it hasn't at all. We were just too busy to notice its passing when we were – remember? -- living life. A reminder, you're over 80 now. The radio or television will almost always be on, if only for a little company, and especially if we live alone. Speaking of media, we'll declare our generation's music to be the best ever, and make every effort to listen to it, because of our intolerance for the music of generations that have followed. Contrary to popular belief, no one, repeat, no one knows for certain what awaits us on 'the other side'. Not your Minister, not your priest and certainly not the one who's figured out a creative way to separate us from our money, and that s/he's the messiah and knows with certainty, all about the paradise that awaits you. Iris Dement sings an unpretentious song called "Let The Mystery Be," and she sings it with a smile. I suggest you do the same, because whatever awaits us, from fertilizer to eternal bliss, there's nothing we can do to change it. But why change it? What we have, here and now, is not a bad deal. We're born, most of us live out our lives, then go headlong into the mystery that awaits us, if any.

Why, some may ask, would this author include ages 1 to 81 and beyond, within a narration that primarily involves censorship and gun ownership? Firstly, it starts small. Remember? But secondarily – and this is most important -- when healthy, the human lifetime is nature's greatest achievement. Again, animals are possessed of most human standards, but animals rely mainly on instinct to survive, and they don't live nearly as long. While humans are mostly devoid of instinct, they more than make up for the shortcoming with compassion, morals and ego, all compliments of the brain. It's the stuff that makes us adopt all those furry little creatures. Within the paragraphs that follow, we'll explore the miracle of the human existence, and why anyone with a gun would be so inclined as to instantly take away the miracle.

2.

I t occurs to your author that we haven't yet asked the question that surely burns in the hearts and minds of his readers. What good would it do to discuss the harm brought about by automatic weapons, when we know little or nothing of the inner miracles that will draw to an immediate close with a single bullet? The human lifetime is a complex mechanism. Good or bad, we all get a body to go along with our lifetime. It doesn't care which side we're on. It just continues to function, for right or for wrong. All of its parts, working in unison is quite the miracle within itself. Medical doctors and medical students are keenly aware of this. What follows is a simplification, perhaps oversimplified in places, of this particular miracle. We'll start at the bottom and work our way up.

A seasoned filmmaker, getting on in years, was once asked, "At what point do you just hang it up, and say goodbye to the art form?" Without hesitation, the filmmaker answered [para] "It's the legs. When the legs go, you're finished." His legs seemed fine to me. He was standing, anyway. Legs, huh? Would that include feet? Because without them, the legs wouldn't be of much use, yes?

Yes. So, you're sitting or laying comfortably, watching a movie or perhaps reading a book, when you decide it's snack time. Without much thought, you get to your feet, go to the fridge, which we'll assume is in the kitchen, wrench open its door and peer inside. What went on during that little excursion, that you knew nothing about?

For openers, your heart continued its rhythmic beat. Kudos to your brain, which, unknown to you, sent a signal to your heart to keep on beating, and usually with no help from you, the owner. Ironically, it's the heart, about the size of your fist, that gets the least amount of concern as you go about your daily life. Why ironic? In the event that the heart stops, everything else stops with it. Game over. While the brain may continue to send messages to the heart to keep on beating, occasionally, with a well placed, oversized bullet, it will beat no more. No more blood to the extremities. No more air in the lungs. No more anything. Your body and all its functions have officially ceased. For all time.

When you decided it's time for a snack, then maybe what the snack should be, and that you'll have to make said snack, a message was sent, again unknown to you, from your brain, replete with about 100 billion neurons, to your legs, to swing outward and down, until both feet hit the cold floor, which you may or may not have anticipated. This, compliments of only one of the five senses we all have. Perchance a pair of slippers was strategically placed, so that your feet could slide right into them, in which case the message went from the brain all the way down to the feet, and with little or no effort on your part. Some call it 'second nature'. In point of fact, your brain was just doing its job, sending a message to the legs and feet. And all the while, tiny white corpuscles are coming together, fighting an infection, somewhere else in your body, that you also knew nothing about. What a miracle!

Back to the movie or back to the book, snack in hand, and all done during the ten-commercial break. Life is good, huh? But wait. During your excursion to the kitchen, you broke the law. In California and other states, the names of which escape me, the manufacture of whole blood, without a license, is illegal, and you're the guilty one. Unknown to you, you manufactured whole blood, without a license. I'm sorry, but if you wish to remain a law-abiding citizen, perhaps you should consider moving to another state. Meanwhile, your secret will be safe with me.

I once believed that only the female human lifetime qualifies as nature's greatest achievement, mostly because, with little or no effort, they're able to procreate. And, as if that weren't enough, after giving birth, they can then feed their young. Most naïve of me. Should men not be included in nature's greatest achievements, just because they can't have babies? Of course not. With the exception of having babies and the menstrual cycle, the male human being contains most of the same miracles to which the female can lay claim. He sees with his eyes. Simple enough. But what he doesn't know about is how his brain translates what his eyes see. Yes, the same can be said of animals, though they tend to have tunnel vision, thus, they only see their enemies, and of course, their friends, not to mention food. Ask any cat.

Within the human lifetime, blood flows through our veins and our arteries, cleansing as it flows; the fingers touch, the nostrils smell, the eyes see, the brain translates, the ears hear, all while the upper and lower digestive tracts are quietly – or at times, not so quietly – doing their job. All in unison. What a miracle! Yet there are those who'd propose to take away these miracles, perhaps with a single shot.

3.

On a warm Summer's day, sometime in the early 1980s, your author was feeling pretty good about himself. As an actor, he'd scored a semi-lead in a not-so-great Neil Simon play called "God's Favorite." What made it great, however, was that the Alda's – Robert and younger son, Antony – would be flying in to 'take control of the performance' about two weeks prior to the showroom opening. Robert, who'd been around for Hollywood's "golden years," would play 'Joe,' the patriarch of the decadent, makebelieve clan, while Antony would play God's messenger (favorite?) Meanwhile, their stand-ins, a guy named Danny and another guy, Ralph, would, you know, stand in.

Somewhere across town, at the same moment, a fair haired young girl of about eight years could barely contain her excitement, while she quickly dressed and found her way to the dinette and breakfast. You see, as a reward for her stellar report card, the girl would later that day, be allowed to pick out anything she wanted, within a reasonable price limit, at the local Toys R Us. Those were the rules: get a good report card, you get a trip to Toys R Us. On this day, the young girl knew exactly what she'd pick out.

We took a dinner break from rehearsal at 3pm. It was one of those day-long, Saturday rehearsals, where everybody gets measured for costumes, and the director makes certain that everyone is off script. Danny, myself and Melany, who played the part of Joe's 'ditsy daughter,' decided we'd dine at the local Sizzler, which was just down the street from the theatre.

The three of us packed ourselves into my old Buick, unwittingly on our way to witness something that would change our lives forever. Dinner was uneventful enough, unless you count the server almost having delivered a second dinner to Danny, for which he promptly proclaimed "Thanks!"

We three then filed out of the restaurant, en route to my car, when we heard a muffled pop, from across the sprawling parking lot. A quick-witted sort, as actors are want to be, Danny clutched his chest, while mimicking, "Ohhhh, they got me." But Melany and I weren't quite as convinced that what we'd heard was a car backfire or firecracker.

"No, wait. I think that really was a shot," I proclaimed, as we all now peered across the sea of parked cars. The camper shell of a small truck sped up one of the aisles, turned a corner on two wheels and came toward us and the only exit from the lot. A woman in the distance screamed repeatedly.

"Someone get the license number," I added, with the small truck nearing. The little Ford truck turned away from us to exit the lot, but had to wait for cross traffic to pass, which is when Danny began to recite the license number, aloud. "Gimme a goddamn piece of paper," he shouted, between the numbers he recited. Melany emptied the contents of her purse onto the hood of my car, hurriedly sifted through it, and came up with the corner of an envelope and a small pencil, which she nervously handed to Danny. We first trotted, then ran toward the feminine screams, all those aisles away.

As he lay flat on his back, felled by single bullet through the heart side of his chest, the once proud Dad's purple blood covered him, the pavement around him and his wife's sleeveless arms. Purple because the blood hadn't had time to be oxygenated (red) before it rushed out of his chest. Knelt beside him, his wife spoke softly, her face now close to his. There was a baby, abandoned by the family, not more than a few weeks old, in a car seat, whose constant wails fell on deaf ears. The straight-A princess stood nearby, frozen in shock at the site of her now dead Father. He'd left behind a wife, a preteen daughter and a newborn baby. All for a parking space.

With the help of Danny's hastily scrawled license number, the shooter was arrested about an hour later. He was someone who'd recently purchased an Uzi, and was anxious to use it. Familiar? Police didn't have to search long for the murder weapon. The shooter'd left it in plain sight, on the passenger seat of the little Ford truck.

That had been only the second time I'd seen a dead person. The first was decades earlier, when a neighbor woman passed in her sleep. The two hardly compared. This girl's Father, an electrician by trade, had suffered a violent death. I've never seen so much blood in my life, before or since the incident, and all from a single shot. When someone buys a gun or obtains it by any other means, the next thing they quite naturally want is to use it. We find out as children, when we can hardly wait to get that cap or water gun home, and show anyone who'll pay it mind, how well it shoots. Thankfully, most of us outgrow that demand.

The need to see the end result of a gun's or bomb's handiwork, is felt, in civilian life, usually by men, who stubbornly refuse to mature. I believe it's called willful ignorance. They remain anxious to end a human lifetime, through whatever means at their disposal. Vladimir Putin comes to mind. He's far removed from the battlefield, but doesn't think twice about ending human lifetimes by the thousands. Especially children. How does someone sleep, with full knowledge that he alone is responsible for the instant, violent termination of human lifetimes?

If any good is to come from the preceding parking lot experience, it is that now you, the reader, can take it from one who's been there, when I tell you that there are no happy endings where a gun is involved. According to Stanford researchers, the odds are 2 to 1 that, with gun ownership, someone will die from pulling the trigger of that same gun.

The fair-haired youthful princess of whom I wrote is surely grown by now, perhaps with babes of her own. At times, I think of her, and wonder if she ever looks back on that day. The day she lost her Father to a single bullet. Forever.

4.

Now, for something completely dissimilar, tho staying within the guidelines of a dictatorship, we'll cover all of the states that have banned books, unless, as with the case of Texas, there are simply too many to list. In the U.S.A., according to PEN America, there are 1,648 books that are officially banned. Between July of 2021 and June of 2022, however, books were banned 2,532 times in public schools across the U.S.A. The state of Texas, as of September 19, 2022, has single-handedly banned 801 of those books, across 22 school districts. The State of Texas, where 1 in 14 people own guns, is also number one in gun massacres. Be advised that the number of books banned may fluctuate almost daily, as so many are added to or taken away from the list. And then some titles, like John Steinbeck's "The Grapes of Wrath," are permanent residents of the list, usually at the top.

Book banning and/or burning was first made public in George Orwell's "1984," which later became a movie, and which, as of 2022, remains the most banned book in America. Not surprisingly, the most banned and challenged book for 2020 was "George" by Alex Gino. Kudos to the author, Orwell, for depicting a future, which is now referred to by many as "Orwellian." That future, some might argue, is now, what with the shenanigans of a handful of politicians and dictators, here on Planet Earth. They find that money and power is all that's needed to command the masses, whether the masses like it or not.

There are three essential reasons for the banning of books in the U.S. Topping the list, at 92.5%, is *too sexually explicit.* Coming in at number two on the list is *offensive language,*with 61.5%, and number three, the *unsuited to any age group* category arrives with a 49% rating. Religious viewpoint (26%), LGBTQIA content (23.5%) and racism (16.5%*) round out the reasons for the banning of books. Enough with the figures, however. Let's begin our list with the states having the most banned books, and work our way down. As mentioned above, the State with the most banned books would be Texas, also 50[th out of 50] in ease of voting. To highlight a few banned titles, in the Lone Star State, we have

"Gender Queer: A Memoir" by Maia Kobabe; "The Bluest Eye" by Toni Morrison; "Roe v Wade: A Woman's Choice" by Susan Dudley Gold, "Out Of Darkness" by Ashley Hope Perez, and "The Absolutely True Diary of a Part Time Indian" by Sherman Alexie. Numbers continue to fluctuate, but regardless of how, or during which time periods, Texas always seems to come out on top. Not sure I'd want to be #1 in this particular parade of fascism. Let's hear it for Texas, where the good ol' boys have contributed, in no small part, to the U.S. now being statistically the least safe country for a woman to become pregnant. More about a woman's right to choose, later.

At number two on our fascist checklist of banned books, we find the State of Florida, land of palm trees, orange juice and hurricanes; land where the Governor, with dictatorial aspirations, and whom at this writing, has seen fit to outlaw any Afro-American studies that might present the Caucasian race in a negative light. Also in the Sunshine State, you can now face hard jail time for promoting any of the banned titles. The number of books banned would seemingly no longer matter, as the list fluctuates so wildly, however, a deal's a deal, and Florida has banned 566 books, and counting.

It seems that, depending on one's political leanings, anything bad always happens in Florida or Texas. My imagination? Not really. As you may remember, I mentioned that the Governor of Florida has 'dictatorial aspirations'. Turns out, as you may have guessed, he'd run for President, and I doubt that I have to tell you which political party celebrates him. He's also put together his own "state guard," at state taxpayer expense, and which has been described by former members, who couldn't get away fast enough, as "another boot camp," to round up all those people who voted illegally. As if that's not enough, in keeping with his now debunked presidential bid, the Governor has also, at taxpayer expense, bussed and flown hundreds of confused migrants from Florida to Massachusetts, all in an effort to make a political point. Of further interest, author John Green's "Looking for Alaska" has been banned in Orange County, Florida, where his mother lives, and where he went to school; the poems of Amanda Gorman, whose poetry, you may remember, was read aloud to a captive audience at a recent Presidential Inauguration, has been banned from public schools by Florida's Governor, this after the required one parent challenge.

Tennessee, birthplace of the KKK, death place of Dr. Martin Luther King, Jr. and of late, the state where two duly elected Black state lawmakers have been expelled for – sin of sins! – partaking in Constitutionally protected, peaceful, civil unrest, regarding gun control, comes in at number three, with 349 books banned.

Number four on the list goes to the Big Sky Country State of Oklahoma, with a significant drop in the number of banned books, at forty three. Author's note: One is too many. Something fascist can be declared about the Governor of almost every southern state, but since time and the boredom of readers is crucial, we'll keep it at a minimum.

Coming in at number five, we have the State of Kansas, with thirty books banned. At number six, we have the State of Missouri with twenty seven books, banned. Number seven would have to be the State of Indiana, home of a former Vice President, with eighteen books on the hit list.

Virginia has banned nineteen books. Virginia is kind of a special case. You see, their current Governor, now with Presidential aspirations, was elected solely on the strength of a TV commercial, which depicted a woman, up in arms over the distribution of a book, which her 'child' might possibly read. Turns out her grown son, and only 'child' had never even seen the book, much less heard about it. Yes, our bodies are quite the miracle. How unfortunate that our brains don't often follow.

In Georgia, the state where so-called conservative lawmakers have passed a new law, which will go into effect in November of 2023, and which will expel (fire) any prosecutor who dares prosecute someone they don't believe should be prosecuted, thirteen books are banned. At last check, it was unknown who 'they' are; the State of New York has banned twelve books and Utah, eleven; North Carolina and California have both banned six books; Washington State and Wisconsin have each banned five books; Illinois, Iowa and Ohio have banned four books each; the State of New Jersey has banned only three books. As already stated, one is too many.

The State of Alaska had banned five books, including "I Know Why the Caged Bird Sings" by Maya Angelou, "Catch-22" by Joseph Heller and "The Invisible Man" by Ralph Ellison. However, due to widespread pressure from local citizens and national groups, such as The National

Coalition Against Censorship, an Alaskan school board rescinded its decision. Source: NCAC.

The State of Michigan has banned two books; the States of Arkansas, Maryland, Minnesota, Rhode Island and South Carolina have all banned one book each. Titles vary.

I urge young people to search out the banned titles in your respective states, and read the books. Not just as an act of rebellion, but because it's important to understand all of our country's history, Black, Caucasian or Native American; because it's important to discover what it is that politicians and school administrators don't want you to see. Is it something about Race? Homosexuality? Slavery? Immigration? Perhaps something historical or concerning the treatment of early Native Americans? Sexually explicit? Maybe something in which the characters use 'off color' language? Whatever it is, you can be sure it's not complimentary to the straight, caucasian, middle-aged, male. Alexandria Ocasio Cortez once once said something that, in this author's opinion, bears repeating. "Studying history will sometimes disturb you, sometimes upset you, sometimes make you furious. If studying history makes you feel proud and happy, you probably aren't studying history."

And by the by, you can relax, your author genuinely promises that if you're caucasian and straight, you won't instantly denigrate the caucasian race or any individual's sexual preference. Children have, but they're young, and will outgrow it. What's your excuse?

5.

In 1957, while your host was watching an eighteen foot tall, black and white werewolf jump off the big screen and into his nightmares, ground was being broken in Hayward, about fourteen miles south of Oakland, for what would become East Avenue Elementary School. The school, which today remains at the same address, is much bigger than when first its front doors were flung open, in September of 1958, and, under the same name, continues to welcome new students.

As an elementary school, East Avenue only facilitated grades K through 4. The following year, when the fourth grade moved on to the fifth, a grade five would be added, and so on, with sixth being the highest grade. Your author would be in grade three. Our principal, Mr. Perry, pulled double duty, as a fourth grade teacher. And yes, corporal punishment was still perfectly legal, and used liberally on 'problem students'.

I had occasion to see Mr. Perry during my adult years, when, as a bartender, I worked a retirement party, given for one of his friends. His coal black hair had since turned snowy white, but, unlike my own, at least it was there. As I poured him a Kahlua and Creme, I jested, "Only teacher who ever gave me the paddle." Oddly, he didn't see the humor. I was again paddled in junior high, where the experience was worn like a badge of honor. In the crowd with which I ran, if you hadn't gotten "the paddle" by the eighth grade, you just weren't doing your job.

During the 1950s, much like today, the State of California paid for all K-6 students' books, paper, pencils and ball point pens, not to mention, also like today, a flat fee it (the State) would pay directly to the school district for each student in attendance, on any given school day. Miss a day and they got no money, hence, truancy was, and remains, of paramount importance. However, there is no more money to pay for what we called "truant officers," whose only job was to round up kids like myself, who'd cut school. Unlike yesteryear also, parents are asked, at the beginning of each school year, to donate whatever they can afford, to a 'book fund' which is for pens, pencils, paper, books, and, of late, bulletproof back packs.

'Duck and Cover', the drill designed, in most schools, to save lives, should a nuclear bomb be exploded somewhere on the West Coast, didn't seem to be an issue. We never practiced it. Closest thing we had was called the 'earthquake drill', whereby the instructor, always out of nowhere, would shout "Earthquake Down!" at which point the previously designated 'curtain monitor' would jump up and close the heavy curtain that was on the inside of what seemed an endless bank of windows, thereby preventing potential flying glass chards from hitting the students.

I have to assume, this being the height of the Cold War, 'authorities' gathered and decided that, should a nuclear weapon be exploded anywhere, we'd all be dead anyway, thus, what good would it do to duck or cover? Except, perchance, making our bodies easier to find, and be carried to the nearest bonfire, none. In our case, however, the nearest big city was San Francisco, across the Bay, ergo, with the exception of nuclear fallout, which would certainly blanket the entire state, we were reasonably safe, solely dependent, of course, upon which way the wind blew.

And while on the subject, let's all get familiar with nuclear fallout, sometimes known as radiation, which was, and continues to be a threat to us all, here on planet Earth. It's delivered by way of a bomb. Not the kind of little bomb I discussed briefly in chapters past, but a big bomb, that would cover, say, the entire L.A. or San Francisco area. The resulting fallout would cover the state, poisoning the ground, so that nothing dares grow or be planted, and the oxygen we breathe. Gas masks required. For about the next hundred years, give or take a few. Rain, which we generally think of as a cleansing agent, would become something to be avoided. Run for cover. You see, if caught in the 'acid rain' your face might melt. Literally. Those who authorize the dropping of the bomb or the missile launch, can't even see the carnage they've effected. But rest assured that, as the fascists they are, they're comforted with the knowledge that they've single-handedly brought about the end of the civilized world. Such a consoling thought that, at last count, there were seventeen countries that are members of the "nuclear family." Imagine the world they'd have created if, instead of concentrating their knowledge and science on weapons designed to kill people by the millions and destroy the planet, they concentrated all their efforts on the betterment of the human race. To help rather than hinder. To offer aid, rather than kill and destroy. To lend a helping hand. I believe it was the afore mentioned Dr. Martin Luther King, Jr., who once said "Those who love peace must learn to organize as effectively as those who love war."

During a recent idle moment, after having witnessed the televised carnage at the Uvalde Elementary School in Texas, which rivaled the mass shootings at Sandy Hook and Parkland, if only in ages of the victims, I wondered about the difference between school attendance in the 1950s, and school attendance in the 2000s. What better place to start than the elementary school attended by your guide, for his early, though not earliest school years, good old East Avenue School? You see, I found it odd that, if asked what s/he wants to be as a grownup, today's elementary school student seems to have a one-word answer at the ready. "Alive."

I suppose the same argument could be made for my own generation. We, after all, wanted to be alive as adults, too. Who doesn't? The difference, however, between my generation and today's school-age generation is that many of these children now have first hand information, as did I, in the parking lot incident, on how a single bullet can mangle the fragile human form. Hence, the 'alive' quip.

My first car trip down the California Coast, on a quest for answers to the 'difference between' questions, was anything but a success. It started successfully enough, but things wound up stifled somewhere on the freeway between Willits and Ukiah, CA, and me at a Motel 6, only halfway to my destination. With another 200 miles to go, seems the alternator, which controls all things electrical in every automobile, decided after fifteen years, that it was time to go. And go it did, never to return. In the far left lane of the freeway, things – steering, brakes, power windows, engine -- just all turned themselves off, kind of like a dead body, the only difference being that a replaced alternator would get the car back on the road, whereas a human body is dead forever.

I managed to get over to the right lane, and parked in the small space that separated the freeway from the off-ramp. With cars whizzing by at 70 and 80 mph, amid record-breaking heat, even for October, I called AAA, gave them the off-ramp number at which I was stranded, and waited for the tow truck, which arrived in about two hours. I decided, later that evening, while cooling my heels at the Motel 6, that if this was a prelude of things to come, perhaps it would be best for me, after getting the car back from the mechanic, to turn it around and head back North, to my home.

My second effort, about a month later, was far more successful. When one is looking in the eye of a 300 mile freeway journey, one's mind tends to wander. Mine was no exception. Related only to my trip South, to visit East Avenue School, I wondered about that staggering, but official statistic that gun violence is the number one killer of children and teens in my homeland. With that in mind, why would Floridian politicians, who call themselves conservatives, float a State Bill that would allow for permitless gun carry in their state? Keeping up with Texas? Here we have yet another situation where logic and common sense, used by rational adults, might prevail. It might. Unless fascism is involved. Then, of course, as the saying goes, all bets are off.

As the road signs flew by and my destination became a shorter distance by the miles, I thought of Miss Smith. Remember the elusive Eunice Smith? She did a huge favor for the third and fifth grade classes at East Avenue School, both of which your host was a member. The class as a whole, was happy that she'd be instructing us in the fifth grade, as we'd already had her tutelage in the third grade, and were envious albeit a bit possessive regarding her instruction to an unappreciative class that was one year ahead of us.

Right, the favor. It's quite simple, actually, though with far reaching implications. Among other things burned forever into my memory, Miss Smith taught us about the evolution of the human race. How it evolved from a single-celled protozoa to what it is today -- the perfect organism – and did it all with nary a word about creationism or the Bible. Good thing, too. During the 1950s and 60s, the church and state were still, for the most part, separate, per the dictates of our Constitution. Although, I'm now told that there are 1600 bills currently tabled by various states, with Texas naturally leading the way, that would effectively bring the church and state together, allowing for such things as prayer in public schools, and recitation of the Ten Commandments to precede each class.

The word fascism, as defined in our trusty dictionary, means "...an authoritarian and nationalistic rightwing system of government or social organization..." Funny how the words stupidity or uneducated are not to be found. 19% per cent of high school graduates, at the moment a diploma is placed in their hands, remain functionally illiterate. And that qualifies the graduate to, oh, start a club, maybe?

There are rules or laws contained within some democracies that may seem fascist, although they're usually propounded by someone who's been arrested on charges that they say are "trumped up." Remember our discussion of the victim? "What does this all have to do with Miss Smith?" you may ask. Without realizing it, on our part and maybe hers, she was preparing us for college. In the fifth grade. Her unabashed lectures regarding history alone, included the treatment of Native Americans by newly arrived caucasians, and literal slave labour. Related to slavery, I wondered if a child was to expected to do the work of a man, at which she snapped, "He did the work of five men."

It couldn't have been easy being gay in the 1950s and early 60s. If we were able, we'd 'just ask Miss Smith' about it, as we were want to do, all those years ago. Couldn't ask her because we knew nothing of the homosexual lifestyle. If you're seven to ten years old, growing up in the suberbs in the early 60s, there is no 'gay' or homosexual. There was, but if gay, you stayed in the closet, and didn't dare step outside that closet. You only know, if you're a boy, that you'll grow up, marry a woman and have a litter of kids, which many gay people did. No such thing as a homosexual man or woman. In point of fact, it was not legal in most states. It remains illegal many parts of the world, including Uganda. I bring up Uganda because it was, and continues to be American evangelical groups, who once made the pilgrimage from our country to theirs, and hit pay dirt. Homosexuality is now illegal in Uganda, punishable by death.

Alas, homosexuality just wasn't a part of our vocabulary, mostly because those of us that were straight knew nothing about it. But Miss Smith did. She gave the impression that might, in this day and age, be considered 'butch,' including, but not limited to the smokey voice and body hair. Thirty five and never married? Hmm. Anyway, I never saw any muscles, tho I know for certain they were there, hidden behind her long, loose sleeves. No matter, we loved our Miss Smith, body hair and all.

A little farther down the highway, I began to wonder, prompted by the "Ten Commandments" law, mentioned earlier, not if, but how much of fascism's tentacles had managed to ensnare our once mostly pure educational system. I guessed it had mostly to do with who was elected to which School Board. Remember all those banned books? When it comes to laying blame, in most cases, you need look no further than your local School Board. Every county has one, and, if you have kids, shame on you for not running for the office of County School Board member. Later, we'll discuss local elections and their supreme importance.

A bit more down highway 101, I pondered the hypocrisy that now seems to permeate the political system of our USA. Don't they realize that it's our constitution that allows them to shoot off their mouths, and, in some cases, get elected, with regard to things they know little or nothing of, and have plans to do even less about? No, it's a whole new crop of Republicans. They just want unbridled power, which brings us back to unbridled fascism.

I'm resigned to the little or nothing that, short of voting I, personally, am able to do. Too old, and probably too cynical to run for office. That given voice, I began to wonder about the situation at hand. Would I be graciously received at East Avenue School? The Unified School District? It is, after all, for a book. Not like I've never written a book. No, I've written two books, neither of which contains the commentary of this work. Hence, the facts and figures, something also not dealt with in previous publications. And as a result, I'm finding procrastination to be my newfound plaything. After penning "In Cold Blood," Truman Capote never finished writing another book. I hope not to follow in his footsteps.

In this age, where the phrase 'logic and common sense' has finally fallen into the hands of conspiracy theorists, who get lots of mileage from it, I find that we, as a civilization, have taken a giant step backwards in the evolutionary process. From cave dwellers to split level home owners, we're nearly incapable of recognizing fascism, without the benefit of swastikas.

Eighty two years ago, the United Nations came together with a single goal, the defeat of fascism. The human race on Planet Earth was intent only on the defeat of one man, Adolph Schnicklegruver, aka Adolph Hitler. After his defeat, for the most part, people throughout the planet danced in the streets. The world had come together to defeat the monstrous being of fascism, though not without a price, especially in Hiroshima and Nagasaki. Millions of lives were lost, The 'Evil Axis' as it was sometimes known, had been defeated. Still, in Germany, Hitler had over a million supporters.

America was not and is not now immune to fascism. Politicians who'd been democratically elected in 1940, in honest and fair elections, were indeed proponents of Hitler and his ideals. Armed with Constitutionally guaranteed First Amendment rights, they spewed their fascist nonsense to all who'd listen. And an audience of thirty million was considerable. Remember, there was no internet, no TV, limited phone use, and 'twitter' was a sound made only by birds. Just newspapers, radio, and if you felt like a movie, there were Newsreels. Still, their audiences, like lemmings, were obedient, and as a result, there was a prolific Nazi underground, right here in the good old USA.

Your historical dragoman once had the misfortune of having been befriended by a one-time member of the 'Hitler Youth'. In his 80s when I knew him, he'd even kept his boyhood uniform. Not a Cub or Boy Scout uniform, mind you, but a Hitler Youth uniform, emboldened with a swastika on each sleeve. Never worked a day in his life. Loved free things. Born into riches – he showed me pictures of his childhood home, which, pillars included, is now a country club – he'd find a rich woman, and live off of her, until she got tired of looking after him, monetarily and otherwise, at which time he'd smooth talk the next unsuspecting damsel. He could charm the leaves out of the trees. What I remember best about him, is how, privately, he'd 'long for the old days', when women were servile and men were authoritarian. When exactly was that?

In a country where a politician can hypocritically promote the adoption of a child, out of one side of his/her mouth, while belittling non-biological Mothers out of the other; in a country where politicians legislate by fear; in a country where computers now ask humans to prove they're not a robot, your humble guide is left to wonder about things like truth, honor, and education, and where it's all gone. If the fascists have their way, will there ever be truth again, or just the hodgepodge of unfinished sentences, of which their proposed leader is only capable? Is a dictatorship what you, the voter, really want?

Many voters are incapable of remembering WWII largely because during and shortly after the war, they weren't yet born. Oh, they studied about it in history books, when they paid attention, but the history books rarely point out human skin that bubbles when roasted, or dead bodies stacked upon more dead bodies, waiting to be covered over with bulldozers. Those particular books have long since been banned. In point of fact, their Mothers probably weren't yet born either. As a result, a country where one man rules the rest of us and declares, anti-Semitically, certain religions to be illegal, sounds like a pretty good idea. Get educated.

In Russia, regardless of who you vote for, the same candidate always seems to win. This was tried in the USA, however, this being a nation of laws, it failed. Most of the seditionists received long prison sentences, and continue to be arrested. You may remember me speaking briefly of it in my introduction. I bring it up again because I don't believe anyone paid it much mind. However, if the seditionists had been triumphant, and if the Vice President had yielded to their demands, the USA, would now be living under a dictatorship.

In a dictatorship, the free press would surely be the first to go. Can't lie to the voters, with a free press, fact checking every word that comes out of your mouth. Certain religions would be next. The Constitution, as we know it, would simply become another piece of shredded paper. In short, we'd be just like Russia. And you, the voter, would cease completely to have a say in our politics. Still think it'd be a pretty good idea? If the answer to my question is "Yes," then so be it. Continue to watch only media which deals in conspiracy theories and requires no verification; to watch and vote for politicians who legislate by fear; to be a white nationalist, aka white supremacist, who a sitting U.S.senator from Alabama now describes as "Good Americans."

It has been proven, beyond a reasonable doubt, that it was Russian money which paid local U.S.media outlets for ads, in eastern states, rich with Electoral College votes, during the 2016 Presidential campaign. Turns out the ads were wildly untrue "facts" about the so-called "Lib" candidate. It worked. Voters bought it, hook, line and sinker, and obediently went to the polls, where they voted to keep themselves "safe." And what did they get? A wannabe dictator, whom, it's also been proven, has the attention span of an intemperate child. But then, he's just what Russia ordered, the

For the record, the "Deep State" and "Antifa" do not exist. And the "America First" slogan has been around since the mid 1930s, popularized by fascists. The 'deep state' was invented by the presidential candidate described in the above paragraphs, who sold it to his followers, who bought it, and as a result, he was elected. But we've been all through this. Anyway, much as it's been told to you, and apparently as much as you didn't listen, Antifa is brief for anti-fascist. You remember fascists. Those guys with swastikas on their sleeves? The guys against whom your great grandfather probably fought, and maybe even died, in WWII? Antifa is a concept, like Mr. Clean's shine in those commercials. There is no organization, no meetings and certainly no president. I only bring it up because I understand they're still looking for the Antifa president. Good luck finding him or her. It might even be the author of this treatise.

You may have noticed, I describe conservatives as 'so-called' or 'self described'. That's because the politicians in charge aren't smart enough to be true conservatives. I've had the misfortune of dealing with real conservatives. Pretty smart bunch. Well-educated and well-versed. Did I mention gentlemen? In short, everything today's political or non-political, wannabe fascist isn't.

6.

T raffic in the small town I once knew as home, was an abomination. Worse even than I'd left it, a few years back. Like ants on an anthill, cars were everywhere. The plan was to check into a motel, then, after all the particulars, probably the next day, head up the hill, to East Avenue School. So as not to make this too much about myself, I won't get too far into the "particulars."

On up the hill, past Hayward High School, and toward my destination, I noticed that the terrain hadn't changed much at all. For a city that grew from a small town to a metropolis during my lifetime, I was kind of surprised that certain landmarks – the Catholic church, the castle, the homes on Second Street – had remained intact. It was like the song says, "Nothing but the dead are dying back in my little town."

Here is where I should mention, for those of you not in the know, that the largest earthquake fault on the West Coast is named for, you guessed it, Hayward, CA. The 'Hayward Fault' runs from the East San Francisco Hills, all the way to San Jose, about 72 miles. As a result, we got "Earthquake Down!" At around three o'clock, when I got close to my destination, I also got a traffic jam. Was something happening that required parental attendance? No. It was the same ritual that happens throughout the country, at about this time. Concerned parents, picking up their children, after the final school bell. A far cry from my own school days, when no one came to pick up Junior, except maybe a lone school bus, available and devoid of riders. On this day in 2023, however, buses were lined up, as if connected by their imaginary tails, and students couldn't board them fast enough. When the bell rang, we, during the 1950s, just went home. Some by bicycle, some by bus, and yes, some simply walked home. Home, to stories of "When I was your age, we walked home from school in five feet of snow!"

We sat in her library, did Stacey and myself, and had a chat. I was careful not to get too far off topic, so stayed within the confines of school days in the 1950s, compared to school days of the present. I did most of the talking, but my edification from Stacey was noteworthy. For the detriment of any terrorists, the "Earthquake down!" drills had become "Stop, drop and lock!" The students were to stop what they were doing, drop to the floor, and the heavy curtain, for which we'd had a human monitor, was now automated, closing electronically, on lockdown. A bit later during our conversation, we were visited upon by a likeable chap, who was introduced to me as the Principal of the school, Mr. Wilson. I offered him a seat, though he declined, saying he was late for another appointment. Anyway, the 'stop, drop and lock' drills happened about once a month. No one knew when. There was something also that kids in my class, for obvious reasons, never saw. Computers. Lots and lots of computers. They were everywhere.

Following our chat, Stacey and I took a stroll around the grounds. My, how they'd changed, usually for the better. The area once known by your guide as "the flats," because it was , well, flat, had, over the decades been paved, and was now marked, with bright outlines of soccer and softball fields. Where I once only saw weeds and snake holes, was now paved over. Still, there'd been many a Little League game played there, and would probably be many more. Played in a few myself.

Though I made no mention of it, having seen the soccer and softball outlines took me back in time, to the year 1961. Your host was in the fifth grade, JFK had just taken the Oath of Office, and our teacher, Miss Smith, charged us with writing a letter to the newly inaugurated President Kennedy. The letter should contain the duties of the President, as well as what we, as ten and eleven year olds, expect of our President, because in those days, our President was someone to whom we could look up.

Miss Smith said that only the letters that she determined to be the best would be included for the President, himself, to read. I was personally thrilled when Miss Smith read aloud the list of students whose letters would be included, because I was on it. Wow, President Kennedy, the most supreme celebrity in the country, will be reading my letter! I couldn't wait to get home and tell Mom & Dad.

Weeks turned to months that went by, so many that most of us, what with the attention spans of ten year olds, had forgotten about our letters to the White House. Then one afternoon, Miss Bryson, the school's secretary, burst through the door, letter in hand. "Excuse me," she interrupted, "but

I have a letter here, from the White House, addressed to Miss Smith's fifth grade class, at East Avenue School."

Miss Smith grabbed the envelope, then turned away, so all we saw was white. Elated, she took a seat, front and center, facing all of us, which had been her usual position when she'd read a story aloud for the class, one of the stories having been "David and the Phoenix," and began to read the short letter that she told us was from JFK's personal secretary, Evelyn Maureen Lincoln.

Curiously, Miss Smith did not pass the letter around, for all of us to see, as was her usual practice. Instead, she packed it away, never to be seen again. The receipt of the letter had made Miss Smith feel so good that she let us all go home early. She was visibly elated – maybe too elated -- perhaps because both lesbians and the CTA (California Teachers Association) had a friend in JFK. Much more of a friend than in Richard Nixon, who stubbornly continued to believe, as did many Americans, that being gay is a curable disease.

I contacted the Kennedy Library, hoping to get a copy of the letter sent to the fifth grade class at East Avenue School, to be included here. But no copy existed. Turns out no such letter had ever been written, much less mailed. It was all a hoax. Miss Smith and Bryson had put their heads together to come up with an elaborate plan that would completely bamboozle our unsuspecting fifth grade class. But why? Most of us had forgotten about the letter writing scheme anyway. Maybe a select few kids, unknown to me, had been bugging her about an answer. I really don't know. Should there be living, anyone who can dispute my findings, I'll not only welcome their belief, but would happily and publicly announce a retraction, and an apology to all concerned. Incidentally, you'll need a copy of the letter.

7.

O ne of the many advantages of having lived as long as I, is that, throughout the years, certain catch phrases may come and go, which, should the creators have had their way, your author won't soon forget. Perhaps they're from TV or radio commercials, maybe from bumper stickers, or maybe they're just something made up, like the movies, from which we got *you're gonna need a bigger boat*. In my own case, fancying myself a writer, whether published or not, most of the catch phrases have been filed away, for use at a later date.

There was no shortage of catch phrases during the late 1960s and early 70s. They were seen everywhere. Be they on someone's bumper or t-shirt, they almost always denoted which side the user was on. *The America: Love it or Leave It* phrase, usually seen on the bumpers of trucks, was one such idiom. Originated by the Teamsters Union, and used to counter an anti-war demonstration, the phrase was short, pointed, and left no guess work, from which "side" the user hailed. Sad that there has to be a "side," but, as earlier stated, it's part of our human culture to pick a side, then become loyal to whichever side you've chosen. Also as mentioned earlier, there's good and there's evil.

The anti-war movement produced many a catch phrase. There was "War Is Not Healthy For Children and Other Living Things" "Draft Beer, Not Students" and, of course, "America: Love It Or Leave It!" to name just a few. Why discuss it? Because it occurs to me that we, as a society, in addition to having taken a giant step backwards, have now managed to go full circle. Seems like only yesterday that it was the fascists, throwing that catch-phrase at us, the anti-war demonstrators. I considered refusal to submit to induction a patriotic act on my part. Like the great Muhammed Ali, if faced with the prospect of involuntary servitude, I'd do it again. But that's not what we're here to consider. It also occurs to me that now we, as patriots, can throw that particular catch phrase back into the faces of the fascists who once popularized it. 'America: Love It Or Leave It!' can now become the catch phrase we patriots can suggest to the fascists, not with a humorous hint, but in ernest. There's Russia, where you can be arrested for no apparent reason, incarcerated, and held without a trial, for pretty much however long they feel like. Or, if Russia's too far to travel, there's always The Philippines, an American territory, where you can be shot by thugs, masquerading as police, for suspicion of dealing drugs, even if you've never dealt so much as an Aspirin. Or, if you're Jewish, how about a pilgrimage back to Jerusalem, where the Prime Minister is currently stacking the Supreme Court with his own partisans?

All of the above countries have one thing in common. They have a fascist dictator. As of 2022, there were fifty seven dictatorships from which you, the unfortunate man or woman without a country, can now choose. And you'll be happy to know that your beloved leader, whomever he is, will be elected and re-elected, regardless of who the popular vote sometimes overwhelmingly favors. He may also be appointed, in which case you, as the citizen, will have no say at all.

After they're elected, using promises they have no intention of keeping, through the use of power, dominance, aggression, and a generous sprinkling of money, none of which ever "trickles down" to the electorate, the dictators mentioned above rule with an iron hand. They wouldn't be dictators if they didn't. Add to the laundry list, cruelty, as in placing a bounty on a pregnant woman and her doctor. They claim that their work is only on behalf of those that elected them. At almost the same moment, they're dispatching thugs to teach all of you lessons that you won't soon forget, unless of course, you're dead. They're kind of like that big, lovable, floppy-eared dog, who stands on its hind legs to lick your face aggressively, and all the while, it's peeing on your leg.

As also mentioned previously, once they're elected, you'll never be rid of them. By one method or another, they'll find a way to worm themselves back into your life. Like fly paper that sticks to your fingers, he'll call you his friend. Unless of course, you don't vote for him. Comes the lesson? King Kong was our friend, but he sure made a mess of things along the way of showing us just how friendly he was.

8.

Shock and surprise will fascinate many more people than will things of grace and elegance. They'll even vote for it. One would have believed, after hearing the 'shocking' contents of the "Access Hollywood" tape, that there's no possible way an idiot, that low in caliber, could get anywhere near the White House. The President is a man or woman to whom we all look up. Put simply, s/he's someone about whom the citizenry collectively says "Wow, s/he's so smart!" and "Not a job I'd want, but thank goodness someone wanted it." Alas, voters were overcome with shock and surprise, and thusly, the American Electoral College – the only one on planet Earth – saw to it that their candidate won the election, and for the four years that followed, Russia had its useful idiot in the White House.

If nothing else, the country learned that fascism can get American votes. The fascist candidates throughout the deep South, with the aid of heavily gerrymandered districts, continue to win elections, even when the opposing candidate gets more votes. That can only mean people – somewhere – still vote for them. Uneducated people? But give credit where it's due, the candidate knew where to look. And once there, we'll talk about 'hot-button' issues, like guns, abortion, book banning, school shootings, and the need to arm teachers, but we'll never talk about fascism, be it subtle or in your face. We'll talk about the need for only one religion, in a country where the Constitution – you know, the one that fascists hide behind for other issues, like gun control – that guarantees freedom of religion. You, the politician, are Constitutionally guaranteed the right to talk about all the things you and your followers want to outlaw. While we're on the subject, should we mention voting rights? Seems it gets more and more difficult just to vote in the Southern states, like Texas and Mississippi.

Now let's deal with mass shootings. In 2020, according to The Kaiser Family Foundation, America had 4,357 mass shootings, while other countries – Japan, The UK, Australia, Germany, Canada, France, et al –

combined to have only 138. Of course, as earlier stated, with regard to the banning of books, one is too many. Mental instability, combined with ease of (firearm) procurement has everything to do with the American mass shootings. So much so, that the Florida Governor has seen fit to slash the budget for mental health, while signing or preparing to sign legislation that would legalize the permitless, open carry of guns. How hypocritical is that? It's one thing to designate someone as developmentally disabled, quite another to put a gun in that someone's hands. But when one is a fascist in charge, apparently anything is okay.

The USA is now statistically the least safe country on the planet for a child to attend school, and for a woman to become pregnant. Looks like the fascists are taking over. Is a political minority, owning and operating the majority, all right with you, the reader? Don't have much of a choice when that particular minority is also in charge of the state and local politics. Should this bother you in any way, no fair complaining, if you didn't vote in the last election. Children are naturally exempt.

Living within the borders of a country that experiences seventeen (17) mass shootings in seven (7) days, sure makes it appear as though some adjustments are in order. To go any further on the subject, I'd have to list the mass shootings, the cities in which they took place and of course, the victims. You, the reader, have doubtless been down that road often, and it wouldn't make much sense to travel it yet again. Besides, American fascism is, as again the saying goes, just too damn hard with which to keep up. Seemingly, you can't turn on a car radio or a TV, or even boot up a computer, without hearing of one or more shocking things done or not done by a fascist politician, to make your life just a little more difficult. Again, as is the case with Tom Tuberville, cruelty is their way.

Whether it's a trip back to the store for something you'd forgotten or picking up your children at school, there's unfortunately no guarantee you'll make it home, alive. That said, let's discuss the odds of you're returning home in one piece. If, perchance, you remember an item that you'd forgotten, while shopping, yesterday, and rush out the front door to get it, you now have officially, a 50/50 chance of returning home safely. I suppose the same could be said about leaving the house for just about any reason. We are, after all, the only animal on the planet that, after a certain age, knows it's going to die. But now, thanks to supermarket, movie theater and elementary school mass shootings, the odds have increased dramatically, that you won't be coming home, or maybe that you will be coming home, but in a box.

On the subject of owner/operators, the NRA, mostly responsible for all the guns on our city streets, owns and operates most of those politicians who made all the promises to you, the voter. The promises that, once again, they have no intention of keeping. When a mass shooting occurs, first, the politicians contend it's too soon, and that we should "Pray for the families and let them grieve." Then, should the subject come up again, perhaps on the floor of the Senate, they throw out the Second Amendment for consideration, of course, with NRA backing. Moderates cower.

In AA and ACA, they talk a lot about 'breaking the chain' of alcoholism. Here, we'll discuss breaking the chain of gun violence. First, a Constitutional amendment. Those require a forty five percent ratification from all fifty states. So what's the problem? In a word, fascism. And, so long as it exists, there'll be no Constitutional amendments. Next, there's voting. Now here's something we can all get our heads around. But wait. eighty million of us didn't vote in the most recent elections. That's how all those fascists got into state and local government. Nobody cared. I'll explain. The states are broken down into counties; then into cities; then, for the purpose of voting, into precincts. The precincts are who elects the school board. If nobody votes, fascism wins. It's as simple as that. A single school board member or local politician has been known to be elected by one vote. Did someone not care?

9.

A U.S. Congressmen and a U.S. Senator, one from Arizona, one from Louisiana, respectively, have called, upon hearing of their messiah's indictment, for a war. I'd personally like to remind those Congressmen that they were both elected in free and fair elections. Free and fair elections that would not be free or fair anymore, should your precious messiah become president. Jeff Sharlet ("The Undertow: Scenes From A Slow Civil War") has said "This is a U.S. Congressman, calling for the real thing." Put simply, we'll be living under yet another dictatorship. Our foreign allies will no longer trust America, which would be considerable. And all because you, Senator and you, Congressman, are unable to recall Normandy and 11,000 deaths, in a fight against fascism.

This would be a civil war, yes? A war between the states? Your friends, with their AR15's, shooting more unarmed people or "soft targets," as you like to call them? I'm non-violent, so you'll have to excuse me from this particular war. Question: What happens when the bullets run out? And, rest assured, they will. Can't go to Walmart for more. Walmart's closed. There's a war on! Oh, and did I mention? Since the Great Civil War, our military has learned to fly. Should be a fairly short war. Maybe two days. Looks like you'll lose. Again. However, there won't be nearly the casualties experienced during the Civil War. But, no getting around it, there will be casualties. Precious lives lost, and for what? Did you kill all the Blacks? No. Did you wipe out all the minorities, who were taking your jobs? No. Kill all the libs? No. Then WHAT?

There's a little something not mentioned when fascists shoot off their mouths about Blacks, Hispanics, Asians, Native Americans and other people of color, supposedly stealing their jobs. I don't even hear it from liberal media. The 'little something' is that those people who they spend all their time hating; those people who work hard for their dollars, and harder for their happiness are all Americans, just like those people doing all the hating.

Getting back to the subject at hand, let's all remember, the states with the highest rate of gun ownership also have the highest rate of gun deaths, including children. I could go on with statistics for hours, but am guessing that, other than a slow shaking of the head, it'd have little or no effect upon you, the reader. Why? Because, aside from voting, there's little or nothing you can do. You could vote the candidate out of office who's owned and operated by the NRA. You had that opportunity in Texas and in Florida, but failed miserably. Wonder if any of those eighty million registered voters that didn't vote in the last election would've made a difference. Guess I'll just have to keep on wondering.

Why choose book bans and mass shootings? Mass shootings are oddly not on the dictator's checklist. Even executions ordered by your future dictator are not to be found, although one woman found herself dangerously close, when, amid chants of "Lock her up!" one fascist Congressional member was heard to proclaim, "She should be shot on the steps of the Congressional Building." The old firing squad, once used to excess by our own military, and still listed, though not used, except in two cases, as a method of execution for traitors and seditionists.

Book bans are a Constitutional no-no. Apparently, there are Governors who believe they can circumvent the Constitution by just entering rules into their own State's Constitution. Mass shootings are a bit more difficult. As mentioned earlier, they are unique only to the USA. In most states, an eighteen year old is eligible for the purchase of anything from a pocket pistol to an AR15, with optional body armor, making more mass shootings probable, an end to which is not in sight. In most of these same states, you'll have to be twenty one to buy a beer, unless the NRA figures out a method by which drunk drivers can be Constitutionally protected. Well, technically, they are, but not in so many words. Since quoting statistics until we're all sufficiently drowsy won't serve to bring back the dead children of Uvalde, nor the high school students of Marjory Stoneman Douglas, or the small children of Sandy Hook, we shan't go there. Instead, we'll concentrate on the parents and siblings of all the murdered children.

I have a sister who's now in her 70s, as is your narrator. Our school days consisted of homework, braided hair on girls and recess. Though, for my sister, there was a fair amount of 'duck and cover' and for me, 'earthquake down' there was never any mention of an 'active shooter' or, if you prefer 'stop, drop and lock' drill. Why? There just weren't any damn active shooters. Yes, there were guns, from which to choose. There was the (outlawed) machine gun, which, as demonstrated in many an old movie, could've done considerable damage. And there was the handsome and reliable six-gun, which only had six shots, and you actually had to pull the trigger for each shot, but which was portrayed "nicely" by all the law abiding sheriffs and private eye's on TV. See, they only shot bad guys who 'needed' to get dead.

I personally have no children, but the parents of today have an insurmountable obligation that I don't believe I'd want. Drop the kids off at school, then worry, with a 50/50 chance that they'll return home safely. This was not said to make nervous wrecks of parents, though your ringmaster would probably be just that.

It's now been proven, among other things, that the Uvalde Police, when presumed to be everything we've come to expect of a police force, failed miserably at upholding the rule of law. They listened to the screams of children being slaughtered, just one thin door away, and did nothing. They heard shots being fired, and did nothing. They were radio'd time and again to excise the shooter, and did nothing. Under Oath, it was discovered that fear was the motivator to do nothing. In other words, they were afraid. In a sense, they can't be blamed. They were up against a lunatic, sporting an AR15, and who knows what his next target may be? In a much bigger sense, the officers take an Oath to protect, defend and uphold the law, regardless of the circumstances, life threatening or not. I won't spend a lot of time denigrating the officers, or what they did or didn't do. For better or for worse, they had their reasons. However, it has to be said that a police department is empowered to serve and protect, and if small children can't rely on the Police for protection, then, who?

Sadly, to make a point that's been belabored, there are mass shootings daily in this, our country. In the interest of time and space, I'm concentrating on the more notable examples.

One of the victims' Father, Fred Guttenberg, Father of Jamie, was present for the sentencing of the Marjory Stoneman Douglas High School murderer. David Hogg, one of many victims, has begun a movement to help people to realize the vulgarities of mass murder, and perhaps vote for the person who will do something more than 'thoughts and prayers' about the current situation. David is young, though he's proven himself a favorable outcome with organizing, having codified a demonstration that attracted hundreds of thousands of people, all with the same concern, younger, older and middle aged. He's also responsible for the groups "March For Our Lives," and "Leaders We Deserve," which both grow daily with memberships. With one of the group's help, David was able to get a Congressional leader elected. Other students of MSD are responsible for groups such as "Never Again."

Nicole Hockley, Mark Barden and Bill Sherlack are all parents and one husband, of the Sandy Hook pre-school massacre. They formed a group readers may have heard about, "The Sandy Hook Promise." The group was organized and came to fruition, about one month after the murders, which, by now you've heard, involved the deaths of twenty children and six adults.

Sooner or later, we'll get a majority in the Senate and in the Congress, who won't be afraid of the NRA and all its money. Unfortunately, as a sign of the times, we'll need a majority in both Houses of Congress, for a 'common sense' statute that would outlaw the AR15 for private ownership. Forever. I'll ask the question that I'm sure has been asked a million times. Does someone really need an automatic weapon, often referred to as a penile extension, to shoot a deer? The answer, for those of you keeping score, is a resounding NO. They need it to shoot people. Remember, it's a weapon of war.

10.

I'd like to take a time-out from bullies and petty tyrants, to say a few words about Sophie Scholl and the White Rose, in Germany of the 1930s and early 40s. Don't know the name? It's okay, I didn't either. Not until I was middle aged. Sophie had a normal, upper middle class childhood. She was a happy, well adjusted child, whose Father just happened to be the Mayor of the small town in which Sophie grew up. When Hitler took control of France and Sophie's brother, Hans, went off to war, on behalf of the Nazis, then came home with first hand tales of innocents slaughtered, her attitude began to change. Having grown up as a part of the Nazi Youth Corps, it was now time to put away childish things and ideologies, including the Nazis.

Sophie'd aspired to attend college and pursue a career in medicine, and was doing just that, when her brother Hans launched the "White Rose," an anti-war group. Their leaflets, usually a one page document, spoke only truth to power. What follows is an excerpt from the White Rose's third leaflet.

"...Our current 'state' is a dictatorship of evil. We know that already, I hear you object. And we don't need you to reproach us for it yet again. But, I ask you, if you know that, then why don't you act? Why do you tolerate these rulers, gradually robbing you, in public and in private, of one right after another, until one day nothing, absolutely nothing remains but the machinery of the state, under the command of criminals and drunkards?..."

Though never confirmed, Sophie is alleged to have pushed a pile of leaflets from a second floor balcony, onto the floor of a mezzanine, where more people could read them. That was her undoing. She was seen by a janitor, who was also a Nazi sympathizer. He turned her in. Sophie's half day trial – if you can call it that – was presided over by the infamous Roland Freisler, who called himself the president of the "Peoples Court." Sophie, Hans and Christoph Probst, another contributing writer, were all executed (beheaded) for the crimes of high treason, the following day. Sophie was twenty one.

A severed head lives on for six to twenty seconds. It is, by far, the cruelest form of execution. They're all cruel, but cutting off someone's head is the peak of cruelty. It gets no worse. One can only hope that during those six to twenty seconds, Sophie remained unapologetic, and knew that what she'd done would be noticed by all the right people, which it eventually was. There is a movie, which I encourage all to see. It was produced in 2005, and is entitled SOPHIE SCHOLL: THE FINAL DAYS. The film stars Julia Jentsch, who quite believably plays the part of Sophie.

While on the subject of heroines, in this present day, it'd be neglectful of your host not to allude to Wandrea "Shaye" Moss and Ruby Freeman. The couple, a Mother and her Daughter, had gotten temporary employment as poll workers in Georgia, for the upcoming 2020 election. However, during that temporary employment, they would become world famous, for all the wrong reasons. I'm sure they'd much rather have received said fame as dancers or poets, than to be singled out by the President of the United States, via his henchman, one Rudy Juliani, as ringleaders of a conspiracy that, it turns out, doesn't even exist.

Seems Ruby and Shaye were photographed, as are all election workers, handing a Ginger Mint between them. Who handed who the Ginger Mint is insignificant, as it only matters that it was handed between them, and caught on camera. Rudy (with a D) assumed the ginger mint to be an official voting document, and ran with it, to anyone who'd listen. Turns out he had a captive audience of one, in the 45th President, who was running out of reasons to stop the vote count, and all who would follow him down. The President used their first and last names often, in an effort to belittle and otherwise invalidate the vote count.

Ruby and Shaye got even by hitting Rudy where he'd feel it most. In the pocketbook. They settled for a $148 million, in a defamation lawsuit, aimed solely at poor Rudy. Next stop, the 45th President. Doubtful that they'll ever see any of the money settled for, but let this be a lesson. Speak kindly of your enemies, unless truth is on your side, lest they come at you with their lawyers. Waydago, Shaye and Ruby!

With regard to Ruby, Shaye and Sophie, the words of Isaac Asimov come to mind: When stupidity is considered patriotism, it is unsafe to be intelligent.

Many of the affairs in question that were paramount in Hitler's Germany of the 1930s, are front and center in the USA of 2023. Let's review: Two members of the U.S. Congress have called for an all out war between the states; some of the most sacred American novels, many of which became legendary films, have been banned from libraries and public schools; just being gay remains illegal in seventy two countries, and is punishable by death in eight of them. While the USA is still not among those countries, you can be sure that if politicians who call themselves conservatives have their way, gay peoples' days are numbered; doctors now fear for their safety or, in some cases, their lives and the lives of their patients, when treating a pregnant woman, compliments of grown men, armed with 'ovulation trackers' and other toys, whose closest encounter with an actual doctor was at their last physical exam; between the NRA, the 2nd Amendment to our Constitution and spineless politicians, the cult of the AR15 and the AK47 is pretty much all sewn up. And now, just for toddlers, there's the JR15! That's no joke. It's a fact.

Now, let's review again, with just a wee bit more depth. While I injected a certain amount of levity in chapters past, here I'll be dead serious. First, to actually name the two lawmakers who've called for a war between the states, would mean memorializing the politicians, not to mention, them seeing their names in print, neither of which I'd care to do at this or any other time. Be assured, however, that they know who they are. While on the subject, if I may interject, as once declared, it's most unfortunate that we Americans must choose a side, and these guys aren't much help. Believing that Americans must take up arms against one another in a new civil war, is ludicrous at best, farcical at worst. HAS IT BEEN SO LONG SINCE THE LAST CIVIL WAR THAT YOU, AS POLITICIANS, HAVE LEARNED NOTHING? Hundreds of thousands died in that war between the states. At times it pitted brother against brother and father against son. There was enough hatred to go around, and it was spread far and wide, never quite mending; blood, and lots of it, was shed, some wounds, psychological and/or physical, never healed. This will be a short war, fought with jets and explosives that have the ability to make firearms of the 1800s look like toys. The side of the haters will lose. Again.

Now let's parenthetically discuss finances. Just being practical, mind you. And directing this squarely at the two Congressmen who'd like to see a war, and maybe secession of your respective states? Do any of your constituents collect or live solely on Social Security? Not any more. You see, Social Security is a federal stipend, proposed in the 1930s, by a U.S. Senator, not a State Senator. Guess they won't be your constituents much longer. Looks like your pension(s) won't make it either, much less the pensions of people who work for corporations based outside of your state.

Moving right along, we have book banning. I discussed this, somewhat at length, in a previous chapter, however, omitted one very important issue of note. The matter of banning books is wholly unconstitutional. Is this not a fascist advance? The removal of a book or books from school and library shelves requires the objection of only one parent. Amanda Gorman discovered that little gem the hard way, when her book of poetry, "The Hill We Climb," one poem of which was read at the President Biden's Inauguration, was banned permanently, based on the objection of one parent in Florida (where else?), by the Governor, who – have I mentioned? – once aspired to be the President. Is that fascist enough for you? What's next? Book burning, perhaps? Be it known that, for every book you ban or burn, five more with the same title will magically come into being. That, among other things, is how Germany lost World War II. This book banning would, however, go hand in hand with the dictatorial policies proposed by some members of the 118th Congress, would it not?

Next, we have being gay. I know I said I would say nothing, but this bears repeating. It's not yet legally punishable by death in this country, it is, but in a much more subtle way. Gay bashings, night club bombings and pickets of children's readings of storybooks via transvestites, by swastika laden Nazis, are at the top of the list. They just can't stand that someone is different. I once saw a TV news story about two openly gay men who'd bought a home, then moved into the home, to start their lives together, in a neighborhood full of straight people. Their neighbors, up in arms, quickly raised a petition to ask the gay men to move elsewhere, which of course, the couple declined to do. The more passive neighbors did and said nothing, while the more aggressive neighbors did things like threw garbage in their front yard, got their water shut off, and one person hit the gay man squarely in the face, bloodying his nose. While I don't know the outcome of the story, the phrase "Live and Let Live" comes to mind, and, for the slower members of our readership, there's always MIND YOUR OWN DAMN BUSINESS! They're just people, like you and I. Just Americans. Get on with your lives, and you may find that gay people will not only get on with their lives as well, though they might offer a helping hand to you. They're not here to harm anyone. Or haven't you bothered to ask?

On the subject of a woman's right to choose, I could write volumes, but will try to keep it short. The recent Supreme Court decision, which hands the choice over to the individual states, and the mostly men running those states, thereby outlawing abortion, is not only unconstitutional (that's two), it's unpopular, among at least 78% of the American populous.

According to the Center for Reproductive Rights, the Guttmacher Institute, the World Health Organization, and Reuters, there are fifty nine countries in which a woman can have a safe and legal abortion. Not that the USA is a member in good standing of that club. We used to be a member, but fascists have seen to it that abortion is now illegal. A woman is an adult human being. She's experienced menstruation, school, and in most cases, the pain of becoming an adult. Regardless of the religious or moral consequences, they are her consequences and no one else's. Even former President Barack Obama, who is on record as being opposed to abortion, has declared the choice of whether or not to end her pregnancy to be a woman's right to choose.For the last time, it's her body. Make it as illegal as you want, and abortions will still happen

There have been a few unintended or maybe intended circumstances to the sweeping abortion ban, since the overturning of Roe V. Wade. The circumstances include women whose doctors are afraid to abort a dead fetus; a ten year old girl, who traveled across state lines, in order to find a doctor, willing to abort her fetus. It's about babies having babies. Amid millions more examples, the right of a woman and her doctor, to privately decide on the woman's well being, has been handed over to politicians.

The States of Texas and Idaho have placed a bounty of $5000 on anyone who assists a woman, in her efforts to have or get an abortion, regardless of the circumstances. This includes doctors, friends or clinics. Hasn't this 'fascist fever,' aimed squarely at women, in a supposed democratic society, gone far enough? As I've said, a fine line exists between fascism and democracy. So fine and so thin that you'll have to take a closer look, just to find the line. Pregnant women and gay people now have something in common. They've both become the property of the government. Gay people, for just being gay, over which they had no voice, and pregnant women, for just being pregnant.

Lastly, but, unfortunately, not the least, we have guns and gun violence. The AR15 figures prominently in this discussion, and might not figure at all, either on network news or amid all the incidental shootings, had this weapon of war never been invented. Since its invention, kids who grew up on fast food and video games, decided that a revolution might be a great idea. Nothing else to do. They have no idea what's written on the Statue of Liberty, much less, why it's even written. "Give me your tired, your poor, your huddled masses, yearning to breathe free, the wretched refuse of your teeming shore. Send these, the homeless, tempest-tossed to me, I lift my lamp beside the golden door" It was written by Emma Lazarus in 1883. You don't really believe that you're the first to shout "revolution," do you? Read on.

American fascists who call themselves 'revolutionaries' and 'patriots' have been around since the early 1930s. It all started with a priest, no less. The 'religious right' found listeners with Father Coughlin, who had a radio audience of about thirty million. During that decade, there was no TV, limited phone use, and certainly no internet or twitter. If you wanted to see a newsreel, you had to go to the movies. Can you imagine the size of Father Coughlin's audience, had there been any one of the above? Speaking of whom, because of his Constitutionally guaranteed right of freedom of speech, the priest had lemmings all over the country, willing to carry out his "divine order," particularly in Boston.

Once upon a time, your host watched an entire insurrection unfold, in the comfort of his own living room. No, not the televised January 6th, 2021 attempt at sedition, which was almost a success, but at a state capitol, where, armed with AR15's, – looks as if they're handing them out to anyone who can afford them -- self styled revolutionaries stood sentry at the State Capitol's entrance, daring anyone to enter. I asked the question aloud, to no particular audience, "Who ya gonna shoot?" Even though the "rebels" have long since been sent to prison, I'd still like an answer to my question. Lawmakers? Secretaries? Security Guards? All the people mentioned who would, without question, be unarmed, even the security guards, and not the least bit able to fire back, especially against AR15's or AK47's.

And with all those witnesses, you'd surely be eventually disarmed or maybe killed. Seems the 'rebels' had also planned to kidnap and execute the sitting Governor of the state, for which, amid other charges,they all received substantial prison sentences.

11.

S elf proclaimed Nazis, waving giant swastikas on flags, have been seen on freeway overpasses in Florida and other states. I wonder if anyone's ever reminded them that it's the very Constitution of this country – the First Amendment, to be precise – that allows for them to make total idiots of themselves. My advice to them is the same advice once given to me, America: love it or leave it. Want a real challenge? In Germany, anyone seen sporting a swastika, be it sewn into their clothing or on a flag, perhaps printed on a leaflet, or spontaneously spray painted on a stop sign, is arrested on the spot and charged accordingly. It's generally the under thirty, willfully ignorant, male caucasian crowd that's seen in the USA with the swastikas. They'll outgrow it, won't you?

The Hitlerian movement has its geographic roots in Southern California. Los Angeles, to be exact. There was a hotbed of Hitler supporters in the L.A. of 1940. They became adept at sending out flyers, at state taxpayer expense, to millions of American citizens. Headed by George Sylvester Verick, who only answered to Adolph Hitler, they wound up in Court. Thirty, in all, flanked by twenty two lawyers, responded to an indictment, charging them with seditious conduct. Many of them even gave Nazi solutes to reporters. The eventual trial was bedlam.

There's been a lot said about socialism and communism, mostly by politicians. About how they fear the dastardly socialism will overtake our country, should their opponent be elected, and in a matter of years, become Communism. Here's the reality: Our local schools, our police department and even our local firefighters, can all find their roots in socialism. Our trusty dictionary defines socialism as "a political and economic theory of social organization that advocates that the means of production, distribution and exchange should be owned or regulated by the community as a whole." It goes on to say that "most European countries, from the late 19th century, have tended toward social democracy." Do we pay city, county, state and federal taxes, in an effort to support our firefighters? I rest my case. Please stop the whining. I'm amused by potential House members, and their naked fear of the dreaded socialism.

When all else fails, raise your voice, which is precisely what the defendants did. They screamed and shouted, so much so, that the judge, who later died while presiding over this case, eventually stood up and walked out of the courtroom. It's also what Clarence Thomas and Brett Cavanaugh, of the Supreme Court did, when things weren't going their way. And it worked. Took everyone's mind off of the subject at hand, and eventually found them a seat on the highest court in the land. Lawyers have a "last resort" tactic, when things aren't looking good, which is to pound on the desk. Sometimes it works, but usually doesn't. Absent the desk, on which we can pound, we have our voice, which we can raise. You may remember, in the film, "To Kill A Mockingbird," when the girl who was allegedly raped by a Black man, had to testify, she simply became hysterical, which in turn diverted attention from the subject at hand, and it worked. Conviction! Although in Brett's case, I believe he also cried. Whatever works, right, Brett?

A group that's only a few years old, the "Moms For Liberty" has seen fit to use a slogan once used by Adolph Hitler, in their letterhead. They're, as you may have guessed, a reactionary group, dedicated to, among other things, the release of recently imprisoned seditionists, as "patriots." There's also the "Blood Tribe," a nazi group, whose leader is retired military.

My overall point brings us back to the unfortunate task of choosing a side. Sad that it's such a necessary evil in our society. Sadder that the utopian world, where the "cops have wooden legs" will have to wait until the afterlife, if any. Saddest that those mentioned here have all chosen the 'side' of fascism, in an effort to actively work against those of us who've chosen real logic and common sense, used ostensibly by rational adults, and would welcome all who'd join us, no questions asked.

Why does one man bully another? Why does one man bully an entire country? The short answer is because he can. The longer answer is that he was well-connected on his way up, had lots of money and a craving for power that refused to be satiated. He gets a taste of power, likes it, and wants more. Yes, some believe his company obnoxious, to a point where he is welcome only in small doses. Notice that I'm only referring to him, because true dictators are always men. Women would seem exempt.

12.

In 1972, about fifty years ago, yet again, there was an American President who aspired, like the 45th occupant of the oval office, to become a dictator. His closest and most conservative colleagues were among the first to inform him of the unconstitutionality of his intentions, not to mention, the illegality. He eventually resigned his Presidency in disgrace, though during his glory years, was referred to, by those in the know, as the "Teflon President" because no charges seemed to stick. Sound familiar?

One might believe that, given their failures at 'political minorities governing political majorities,' they might try a different approach. But no, they haven't learned a thing. Failure only gives rise to more failure. It requires no super intelligent person to quote the previous phrase. Only a generous dose of logic and common sense. There are thousands of phrases just like it. Although, fifty years ago, at least the conservatives were willing to adhere to the Constitution. Now, it's just a free-for-all. A contest, if you will, to see who can out-fascist the other.

They regrouped in 2012. Apparently, that was just a dress rehearsal for current times. It all reminds your guide of a song, the lyrics of which were popular in the 1960s. "And if you go chasing rabbits, and you know you're going to fall..." The song goes on to set forth, "When logic and proportion have fallen sloppy dead..." Remember what the dormouse said!

The average age of the Founding Fathers, at the signing of our Declaration of Independence, on July 4, 1776, was forty. Andrew Jackson was only nine (9). During that era, life expectancy for the average male was about thirty five (35). We've come a long way with life extending medical technology since then, hence the average age reached by men, as of 2021, is seventy three (73), and by women, seventy nine (79). At the signing party of the Declaration, the men were made to look much older, as shown in portraits done by Gilbert Stuart and others, what with white wigs and white powder to enhance the wigs. Indeed, given the age of signatories, the the gathering might have been better known as the "Founding Teenagers" or "Twenty Somethings." Over half of the Founding Fathers were under forty.

I bring this up because, like the professional athletes of today, these men were in their prime. They held the future of thirteen colonies within the palms of their signing hands. They were considered radicals for their time, having been literally thrown out of their respective countries of origin. And yes, contrary to what 'white supremacists' may believe, we in the USA are a nation of immigrants. As such, these revolutionaries had radical ideals, such as allowing any person, regardless of color, to become a citizen. What follows are copies of both the Declaration of Independence and The U.S. Constitution. Feel free to bookmark it for a handy reference.

(Painting of Founding Fathers)
others: "Our Founding Fathers"

It was Thomas Edison, whose biggest fear, as he threw the switch that electronically lit up the city of New York for the first time, that technology would morally and scientifically outrun the human race. A good cinematic example is "Colossus: The Forbin Project." In 2023 we're realizing Tom Edison's worst nightmare. While medical advances have served us well, and are too numerous to count, technological advances such as artificial intelligence or "AI" have pulled us into an abyss.

An example of the Edison nightmare was realized by your guide, during a recent electrical blackout. It lasted for five days, during which people were helpful enough, though tragically unprepared for the major setback that befell them. The local power company set up 'charging stations' for those with cell phones. The stations were swamped. I personally found myself becoming short-fused and emotional when the sun went down. During frontier days, people had no electricity, and organized their daily lives around it. They went to bed early and rode horses before there were cars to drive. They lit their homes with kerosene, as a light bulb was way in their faraway future. And with no refrigeration, their vegetables and meats managed to stay pure.

People say "Look to the future," but, to a certain extent, it's best to stop and enjoy what we have, before moving on. Meanwhile, corporations pay millions upon millions of dollars for employees to come up with new and "improved" ways to make our lives easier.

Yes, it's true that the solar powered automobile is about forty years late, and, yes, was first perfected in the mid 1970s, though during that time, there were millions of people who collectively said "Hold on a minute!" Those people were the workers of the UAW and their families. Workers who relied upon General Motors, Chrysler or Ford, for their livelihood, and had no other skills. The electric vehicle, also about fifty years late, has enjoyed recent popularity, but for most is cost prohibitive.

It's now possible for an entire feature length motion picture to be made from the confines of a desktop computer. Characters, dialogue, music, sound effects, and titles, all of it are compliments of the desktop, for those who know the keystrokes. It's where AI makes its grand entry. Remember my stating that it has pulled us into an abyss. Do you pay money to see a film? Of course you do, though your payment to cable companies, for watching said movies in the privacy of your home, is much more subtle. Do you buy popcorn to enjoy during the film? Maybe.

Either way, the big studio now has your money. The theater only makes money from popcorn, soda and candy sales. Your admission price goes to the studio. Having been a filmmaker myself, I can assure you that all of this is true.

So, where does your money go? Oddly, big studios seldom spend their own money on such paltry things as film production. It's an all-or-nothing proposition. They either finance the entire film or none of it. This is where the "outside investors" come in. If the film makes tens of millions of dollars, the investors laugh all the way to the bank. If not, they've thrown their money away, and can usually afford it. It is with the latter that we'll concern ourselves, because that's where AI makes its, as stated, grand entry.

AI is able to fashion a character from an actual human being, sometimes a known actor, recreate the character's voice and movement, add music and, of course, explosions, and we've got a movie. You're now $10 poorer, or however much it took to get you to your couch or through the turnstile. Film, while an optional time killer, is a perfect example of the biggest fear harbored by Thomas Edison.

"The sacred rights of mankind are not to be rummaged for, among old parchments, or musty records. They are written, as with a sun beam in the whole volume of human nature, by the hand of the divinity itself; and can never be erased or obscured by mortal power."

— Alexander Hamilton, 1775

"The basis of our political systems is the right of the people to make and to alter their Constitutions of Government. But the Constitution which at any time exists, 'till changed by an explicit and authentic act of the whole People is sacredly obligatory upon all."

— George Washington, 1796

"The Declaration of Independence...[is the] declaratory charter of our rights, and of the rights of man."

— Thomas Jefferson, 1819

THE DECLARATION OF INDEPENDENCE

Action of Second Continental Congress, July 4, 1776

The Unanimous Declaration of the thirteen united States of America

When in the Course of human Events, it becomes necessary for one People to dissolve the Political Bands which have connected them with another, and to assume among the Powers of the Earth, the separate and equal Station to which the Laws of Nature and of Nature's God entitle them, a decent Respect to the Opinions of Mankind requires that they should declare the causes which impel them to the Separation.

We hold these Truths to be self-evident, that all Men are created equal, that they are endowed by their Creator with certain unalienable Rights, that among these are Life, Liberty, and the pursuit of Happiness— That to secure these Rights, Governments are instituted among Men, deriving their just Powers from the Consent of the Governed, that whenever any Form of Government becomes destructive of these Ends, it is the Right of the People to alter or to abolish it, and to institute new Government, laying its Foundation on such Principles, and organizing its Powers in such Form, as to them shall seem most likely to effect their Safety and Happiness. Prudence, indeed, will dictate that Governments long established should not be changed for light and transient Causes; and accordingly all Experience hath shewn, that Mankind are more disposed to suffer, while Evils are sufferable, than to right themselves by abolishing the Forms to which they are accustomed. But when a long Train of Abuses and Usurpations, pursuing invariably the same Object, evinces a design to reduce them under absolute Despotism, it is their Right, itis their Duty, to throw off such Government, and to provide new Guards for their future Security. Such has been the patient Sufferance of these Colonies; and such is now the Necessity which constrains them to alter their former Systems of Government. The History of the present King of Great-Britain is a History of repeated Injuries and Usurpations, all having in direct Object the Establishment of an absolute Tyranny over these States. To prove this, let Facts be submitted to a candid World.

He has refused his Assent to Laws, the most wholesome and necessary for the public Good.

He has forbidden his Governors to pass Laws of immediate and pressing Importance, unless suspended in their Operation till his Assent should be obtained; and when so suspended, he has utterly neglected to attend to them.

He has refused to pass other Laws for the Accommodation of large

Districts of People, unless those People would relinquish the Right of Representation in the Legislature, a Right inestimable to them, and formidable to Tyrants only.

He has called together Legislative Bodies at Places unusual, uncomfortable, and distant from the Depository of their public Records, for the sole Purpose of fatiguing them into Compliance with his Measures.

He has dissolved Representative Houses repeatedly, for opposing with manly Firmness his Invasions on the Rights of the People.

He has refused for a long Time, after such Dissolutions, to cause others to be elected; whereby the Legislative Powers, incapable of Annihilation, have returned to the People at large for their exercise; the State remaining in the mean time exposed to all the Dangers of Invasion from without, and Convulsions within.

He has endeavoured to prevent the Population of these States; for that Purpose obstructing the Laws for Naturalization of Foreigners; refusing to pass others to encourage their Migrations hither, and raising the Conditions of new Appropriations of Lands.

He has obstructed the Administration of Justice, by refusing his Assent to Laws for establishing Judiciary Powers.

He has made Judges dependent on his Will alone, for the Tenure of their Offices, and the Amount and Payment of their Salaries.

He has erected a Multitude of new Offices, and sent hither Swarms of Officers to harrass our People, and eat out their Substance.

He has kept among us, in Times of Peace, Standing Armies, without the consent of our Legislatures.

He has affected to render the Military independent of and superior to the Civil Power.

He has combined with others to subject us to a Jurisdiction foreign to our Constitution, and unacknowledged by our Laws; giving his Assent to their Acts of pretended Legislation:

For quartering large Bodies of Armed Troops among us:

For protecting them, by a mock Trial, from Punishment for any Murders which they should commit on the Inhabitants of these States:

For cutting off our Trade with all Parts of the World:

For imposing Taxes on us without our Consent:

For depriving us, in many Cases, of the Benefits of Trial by Jury:

For transporting us beyond Seas to be tried for pretended Offences:

For abolishing the free System of English Laws in a neighbouring Province, establishing therein an arbitrary Government, and enlarging its Boundaries, so as to render it at once an Example and fit Instrument for introducing the same absolute Rule into these Colonies:

For taking away our Charters, abolishing our most valuable Laws, and altering fundamentally the Forms of our Governments:

For suspending our own Legislatures, and declaring themselves invested with Power to legislate for us in all Cases whatsoever.

He has abdicated Government here, by declaring us out of his Protection and waging War against us.

He has plundered our Seas, ravaged our Coasts, burnt our Towns, and destroyed the Lives of our People.

He is, at this Time, transporting large Armies of foreign Mercenaries to compleat the Works of Death, Desolation, and Tyranny, already begun with circumstances of Cruelty and Perfidy, scarcely paralleled in the most barbarous Ages, and totally unworthy the Head of a civilized Nation.

He has constrained our fellow Citizens taken Captive on the high Seas to bear Arms against their Country, to become the Executioners of their Friends and Brethren, or to fall themselves by their Hands.

He has excited domestic Insurrections amongst us, and has endeavoured to bring on the Inhabitants of our Frontiers, the merciless Indian Savages, whose known Rule of Warfare, is an undistinguished Destruction of all Ages, Sexes and Conditions.

In every stage of these Oppressions we have Petitioned for Redress in the most humble Terms: Our repeated Petitions have been answered only by

repeated Injury. A Prince, whose Character is thus marked by every act which may define a Tyrant, is unfit to be the Ruler of a free People.

Nor have we been wanting in Attentions to our British Brethren. We have warned them from Time to Time of Attempts by their Legislature to extend an unwarrantable Jurisdiction over us. We have reminded them of the Circumstances of our Emigration and Settlement here. We have appealed to their native Justice and Magnanimity, and we have conjured them by the Ties of our common Kindred to disavow these Usurpations, which,would inevitably interrupt our Connections andCorrespondence. They too have been deaf to theVoice of Justice and of Consanguinity. We must,therefore, acquiesce in the Necessity, whichdenounces our Separation, and hold them, as we hold the rest of Mankind, Enemies in War, in Peace, Friends.

We, therefore, the Representatives of the united *States of America,* in General Congress, Assembled, appealing to the Supreme Judge of the World for the Rectitude of our Intentions, do, in the Name, and by Authority of the good People of these Colonies, solemnly Publish and Declare, That these United Colonies are, and of Right ought to be Free and Independent States; that they are absolved from all Allegiance to the

British Crown, and that all political Connection between them and the State of Great-Britain, is and ought to be totally dissolved; and that as *Free and Independent States,* they have full Power to levy War, conclude Peace, contract Alliances, establish Commerce, and to do all other Acts and Things which *Independent States* may of right do. —And for the support of this Declaration, with a firm Reliance on the Protection of divine Providence, we mutually pledge to each other our Lives, our Fortunes, and our sacred Honor.

Signed by ORDER and in BEHALF of the CONGRESS,

John Hancock, President

Attest.
Charles Thomson, Secretary

Signers of the Declaration of Independence

Georgia:
Button Gwinnett
Lyman Hall
George Walton
North Carolina:
William Hooper
Joseph Hewes
John Penn
South Carolina:
Edward Rutledge
Thomas Heyward, Jr.
Thomas Lynch, Jr.
Arthur Middleton
Massachusetts:
Samuel Adams
John Adams
Robert Treat Paine
Elbridge Gerry
John Hancock
Maryland:
Samuel Chase
William Paca
Thomas Stone
Charles Carroll of Carrollton
Virginia:
George Wythe
Richard Henry Lee
Thomas Jefferson
Benjamin Harrison
Thomas Nelson, Jr.
Francis Lightfoot Lee
Carter Braxton
Pennsylvania:
Robert Morris
Benjamin Rush

Benjamin Franklin
John Morton
George Clymer
James Smith
George Taylor
James Wilson
George Ross
Delaware:
Caesar Rodney
George Read
Thomas McKean
New York:
William Floyd
Philip Livingston
Francis Lewis
Lewis Morris
New Jersey:
Richard Stockton
John Witherspoon
Francis Hopkinson
John Hart
Abraham Clark
New Hampshire:
Josiah Bartlett
Matthew Thornton
William Whipple
Rhode Island:
Stephen Hopkins
William Ellery
Connecticut:
Roger Sherman
Samuel Huntington
William Williams
Oliver Wolcott

THE CONSTITUTION
OF THE UNITED STATES OF AMERICA

We the People of the United States, in Order to form a more perfect Union, establish Justice, insure domestic Tranquility, provide for the common defence, promote the general Welfare, and secure the Blessings of Liberty to ourselves and our Posterity, do ordain and establish this Constitution for the United States of America.

Article. I

Section. 1. All legislative Powers herein granted shall be vested in a Congress of the United States, which shall consist of a Senate and house of Representatives.

Section. 2. The house of Representatives shall be composed of Members chosen every second Year by the People of the several States, and the Electors in each State shall have the Qualifications requisite for electors of the most numerous Branch of the State Legislature.

No Person shall be a Representative who shall not have attained to the Age of twenty five Years, and been seven Years a Citizen of the United States, and who shall not, when elected, be an Inhabitant of that State in which he shall be chosen.

[Representatives and direct Taxes shall be apportioned among the several States which may be included within this Union, according to their respective Numbers, which shall be determined by adding to the whole Number of free Persons, including those bound to Service for a Term of Years, and excluding Indians not taxed, three fifths of all other Persons.][1] The actual enumeration shall be made within three Years after the first Meeting of the Congress of the United States, and within every subsequent Term of ten Years, in such Manner as they shall by Law direct. The number of Representatives shall not exceed one for every thirty Thousand, but each State shall have at Least one Representative; and until such enumeration shall be made, the State of New hampshire shall be entitled to chuse three, Massachusetts eight, Rhode-Island and Providence Plantations one, Connecticut five, New-York six, New Jersey four, Pennsylvania eight, Delaware one, Maryland six, Virginia ten, North Carolina five, South Carolina five, and Georgia three.

---

[1] Changed by section 2 of the Fourteenth Amendment.

When vacancies happen in the Representation from any State, the executive Authority thereof shall issue Writs of Election to fill such Vacancies.

The house of Representatives shall chuse their Speaker and other Officers; and shall have the sole Power of Impeachment.

Section. 3. The Senate of the United States shall be composed of two Senators from each State, [chosen by the Legislature thereof,][2] for six Years; and each Senator shall have one Vote.

Immediately after they shall be assembled in Consequence of the first Election, they shall be divided as equally as may be into three Classes. The Seats of the Senators of the first Class shall be vacated at the expiration of the second Year, of the second Class at the expiration of the fourth Year, and of the third Class at the expiration of the sixth Year, so that one third may be chosen every second Year; [and if Vacancies happen by Resignation, or otherwise, during the Recess of the Legislature of any State, the executive thereof may make temporary Appointments until the next Meeting of the Legislature, which shall then fill such Vacancies.][3]

No Person shall be a Senator who shall not have attained to the Age of thirty Years, and been nine Years a Citizen of the United States, and who shall not, when elected, be an Inhabitant of that State for which he shall be chosen.

The Vice President of the United States shall be President of the Senate, but shall have no Vote, unless they be equally divided.

The Senate shall chuse their other Officers, and also a President pro tempore, in the Absence of the Vice President, or when he shall exercise the Office of President of the United States.

The Senate shall have the sole Power to try all Impeachments. When sitting for that Purpose, they shall be on Oath or Affirmation.When the President of the United States is tried, the Chief Justice shall preside: And no Person shall be convicted without the Concurrence of two thirds of the Members present.

Judgment in Cases of Impeachment shall not extend further than to removal from Office, and disqualification to hold and enjoy any Office of honor, Trust or Profit under the United States: but the Party convicted shall nevertheless be liable and subject to Indictment, Trial, Judgment and Punishment, according to Law.

---

[2]Changed by the Seventeenth Amendment.

[3]Changed by the Seventeenth Amendment.

Section. 4. The Times, Places and Manner of holding elections for Senators and Representatives, shall be prescribed in each State by the Legislature thereof; but the Congress may at any time by Law make or alter such Regulations, except as to the Places of chusing Senators.

The Congress shall assemble at least once in every Year, and such Meeting shall be [on the first Monday in December,][4] unless they shall by Law appoint a different Day.

Section. 5. each house shall be the Judge of the Elections, Returns and Qualifications of its own Members, and a Majority of each shall constitute a Quorum to do Business; but a smaller Number may adjourn from day to day, and may be authorized to compel the Attendance of absent Members, in such Manner, and under such Penalties as each house may provide.

Each house may determine the Rules of its Proceedings, punish its Members for disorderly Behaviour, and, with the Concurrence of two thirds, expel a Member.

Each house shall keep a Journal of its Proceedings, and from time to time publish the same, excepting such Parts as may in their Judgment require Secrecy; and the Yeas and Nays of the Members of either house on any question shall, at the Desire of one fifth of those Present, be entered on the Journal.

Neither house, during the Session of Congress, shall, without the Consent of the other, adjourn for more than three days, nor to any other Place than that in which the two houses shall be sitting.

Section. 6. The Senators and Representatives shall receive a Compensation for their Services, to be ascertained by Law, and paid out of the Treasury of the United States. They shall in all Cases, except Treason, Felony and Breach of the Peace, be privileged from Arrest during their Attendance at the Session of their respective houses, and in going to and returning from the same; and for any Speech or Debate in either house, they shall not be questioned in any other Place.

No Senator or Representative shall, during the Time for which he was elected, be appointed to any civil Office under the Authority of the United States, which shall have been created, or the emoluments whereof shall have been increased during such time; and no Person holding any Office under the United States, shall be a Member of either house during his Continuance in Office.

---

[4]Changed by section 2 of the Twentieth Amendment.

Section. 7. All Bills for raising Revenue shall originate in the house of Representatives; but the Senate may propose or concur with Amendments as on other Bills.

every Bill which shall have passed the house of Representatives and the Senate, shall, before it become a Law, be presented to the President of the United States; If he approve he shall sign it, but if not he shall return it, with his Objections to that house in which it shall have originated, who shall enter the Objections at large on their

Journal, and proceed to reconsider it. If after such Reconsideration two thirds of that house shall agree to pass the Bill, it shall be sent, together with the Objections, to the other house, by which it shall likewise be reconsidered, and if approved by two thirds of that house, it shall become a Law. But in all such Cases the Votes of both houses shall be determined by yeas and Nays, and the Names of the Persons voting for and against the Bill shall be entered on the Journal of each house respectively. If any Bill shall not be returned by the President within ten Days (Sundays excepted) after it shall have been presented to him, the Same shall be a Law, in like Manner as if he had signed it, unless the Congress by their Adjournment prevent its Return, in which Case it shall not be a Law.

Every Order, Resolution, or Vote to which the Concurrence of the Senate and house of Representatives may be necessary (except on a question of Adjournment) shall be presented to the President of the United States; and before the Same shall take effect, shall be approved by him, or being disapproved by him, shall be repassed by two thirds of the Senate and house of Representatives, according to the Rules and Limitations prescribed in the Case of a Bill.

Section. 8. The Congress shall have Power To lay and collect Taxes, Duties, Imposts and excises, to pay the Debts and provide for the common Defence and general Welfare of the United States; but all Duties, Imposts and excises shall be uniform throughout the United States;

To borrow Money on the credit of the United States;

To regulate Commerce with foreign Nations, and among the several States, and with the Indian Tribes;

To establish an uniform Rule of Naturalization, and uniform Laws on the subject of Bankruptcies throughout the United States;

To coin Money, regulate the Value thereof, and of foreign Coin, and fix the Standard of Weights and Measures;

To provide forthe Punishment ofcounterfeiting the Securities and current Coin of the United States;

To establish Post Offices and post Roads;

To promote the Progress of Science and useful Arts, by securing for limited Times to Authors and Inventors the exclusive Right to their respective Writings and Discoveries;

To constitute Tribunals inferior to the supreme Court;

To define and punish Piracies and Felonies committed on the high Seas, and Offences against the Law of Nations;

To declare War, grant Letters of Marque and Reprisal, and make Rules concerning Captures on Land and Water;

To raise and support Armies, but no Appropriation of Money to that Use shall be for a longer Term than two Years;

To provide and maintain a Navy;

To make Rules for the Government and Regulation of the land and naval Forces;

To provide forcallingforththe Militiatoexecute the Laws of the Union, suppress Insurrections and repel Invasions;

To provide for organizing, arming, and disciplining, the Militia, and for governing such Part of them as may be employed in the Service of the United States, reserving to the States respectively, the Appointment of the Officers, and the Authority of training the Militia according to the discipline prescribed by Congress;

To exercise exclusive Legislation in all Cases whatsoever, over such District (not exceeding ten Miles square) as may, by Cession of particular States, and the Acceptance of Congress, become the Seat of the Government of the United States, and to exercise like Authority over all Places purchased by the Consent of the Legislature of the State in which the Same shall be, for the erection of Forts, Magazines, Arsenals, dock-Yards, and other needful Buildings;—And

To make all Laws which shall be necessary and proper for carrying into execution the foregoing Powers, and all other Powers vested by this Constitution in the Government of the United States, or in any Department or Officer thereof.

Section. 9. The Migration or Importation of such Persons as any of the States now existing shall think proper to admit, shall not be prohibited by the Congress prior to the Year one thousand eight hundred and eight, but a Tax or duty may be imposed on such Importation, not exceeding ten dollars for each Person.

The Privilege of the Writ of habeas Corpus shall not be suspended, unless when in Cases of Rebellion or Invasion the public Safety may require it.

No Bill of Attainder or ex post facto Law shall be passed.

No Capitation, or other direct,Tax shall be laid, unless in Proportion to the Census or enumeration herein before directed to be taken.[5]

No Tax or Duty shall be laid on Articles exported from any State.

No Preference shall be given by any Regulation of Commerce or Revenue to the Ports of one State over those of another: nor shall Vessels bound to, or from, one State, be obliged to enter, clear, or pay Duties in another.

No Money shall be drawn from the Treasury, but in Consequence of Appropriations made by Law; and a regular Statement and Account of the Receipts and expenditures of all public Money shall be published from time to time.

No Title of Nobility shall be granted by the United States: And no Person holding any Office of Profit or Trust under them, shall, without the Consent of the Congress, accept of any present, Emolument, Office, or Title, of any kind whatever, from any King, Prince, or foreign State.

Section. 10. No State shall enter into anyTreaty, Alliance, or Confederation; grant Letters of Marque and Reprisal; coin Money; emit Bills of Credit; make any Thing but gold and silver Coin a Tender in Payment of Debts; pass any Bill of Attainder, ex post facto Law, or Law impairing the Obligation of Contracts, or grant any Title of Nobility.

No State shall, without the Consent of the Congress, lay any Imposts or Duties on Imports or exports, except what may be absolutely necessary for executing it's inspection Laws: and the net Produce of all Duties and Imposts, laid by any State on Imports or exports, shall be for the Use of the Treasury of the United States; and all such Laws shall be subject to the Revision and Controul of the Congress.

No State shall, without the Consent of Congress, lay any Duty of Tonnage, keep Troops, or Ships of War in time of Peace, enter into any Agreement or Compact with another State, or with a foreign Power, or engage in War, unless actually invaded, or in such imminent Danger as will not admit of delay.

---

[5]See the Sixteenth Amendment.

Article. II.

Section. 1. The executive Power shall be vested in a President of the United States of America. he shall hold his Office during the Term of four Years, and, together with the Vice President, chosen for the same Term, be elected, as follows:

Each State shall appoint, in such Manner as the Legislature thereof may direct, a Number of electors, equal to the whole Number of Senators and Representatives to which the State may be entitled in the Congress: but no Senator or Representative, or Person holding an Office of Trust or Profit under the United States, shall be appointed an elector.

[The electors shall meet in their respective States, and vote by Ballot for two Persons, of whom one at least shall not be an Inhabitant of the same State with themselves. And they shall make a List of all the Persons voted for, and of the Number of Votes for each; which List they shall sign and certify, and transmit sealed to the Seat of the Government of the United States, directed to the President of the Senate. The President of the Senate shall, in the Presence of the Senate and house of Representatives, open all the Certificates, and the Votes shall then be counted. The Person having the greatest Number of Votes shall be the President, if such Number be a Majority of the whole Number of electors appointed; and if there be more than one who have such Majority, and have an equal Number of Votes, then the house of Representatives shall immediately chuse by Ballot one of them for President; and if no Person have a Majority, then from the five highest on the List the said House shall in like Manner chuse the President. But in chusing the President, the Votes shall be taken by States, the Representation from each State having one Vote; A quorum for this Purpose shall consist of a Member or Members from two thirds of the States, and a Majority of all the States shall be necessary to a Choice. In every Case, after the Choice of the President, the Person having the greatest Number of Votes of the electors shall be the Vice President. But if there should remain two or more who have equal Votes, the Senate shall chuse from them by Ballot the Vice President.][6]

The Congress may determine the Time of chusing the electors, and the Day on which they shall give their Votes; which Day shall be the same throughout the United States.

---

[6]Changed by the Twelfth Amendment.

No Person except a natural born Citizen, or a Citizen of the United States, at the time of the Adoption of this Constitution, shall be eligible to the Office of President; neither shall any Person be eligible to that Office who shall not have attained to the Age of thirty five Years, and been fourteen Years a Resident within the United States.

[In Case of the Removal of the President from Office, or of his Death, Resignation, or Inability to discharge the Powers and Duties of the said Office, the Same shall devolve on the Vice President, and the Congress may by Law provide for the Case of Removal, Death, Resignation or Inability, both of the President and Vice President, declaring what Officer shall then act as President, and such Officer shall act accordingly, until the Disability be removed, or a President shall be elected.][7]

The President shall, at stated Times, receive for his Services, a Compensation, which shall neither be increased nor diminished during the Period for which he shall have been elected, and he shall not receive within that Period any other emolument from the United States, or any of them.

Before he enter on the Execution of his Office, he shall take the following Oath or Affirmation:—"I do solemnly swear (or affirm) that I will faithfully execute the Office of President of the United States, and will to the best of my Ability, preserve, protect and defend the Constitution of the United States."

Section. 2. The President shall be Commander in Chief of the Army and Navy of the United States, and of the Militia of the several States, when called into the actual Service of the United States; he may require the Opinion, in writing, of the principal Officer in each of the executive Departments, upon any Subject relating to the Duties of their respective Offices, and he shall have Power to grant Reprieves and Pardons for Offences against the United States, except in Cases of Impeachment.

He shall have Power, by and with the Advice and Consent of the Senate, to make Treaties, provided two thirds of the Senators present concur; and he shall nominate, and by and with the Advice and Consent of the Senate, shall appoint Ambassadors, other public Ministers and Consuls, Judges of the supreme Court, and all other Officers of the United States, whose Appointments are not herein otherwise provided for, and

---

[7]Changed by the Twenty-Fifth Amendment.

which shall be established by Law: but the Congress may by Law vest the Appointment of such inferior Officers, as they think proper, in the President alone, in the Courts of Law, or in the heads of Departments.

The President shall have Power to fill up all Vacancies that may happen during the Recess of the Senate, by granting Commissions which shall expire at the end of their next Session.

Section. 3. he shall from time to time give to the Congress Information of the State of the Union, and recommend to their Consideration such Measures as he shall judge necessary and expedient; he may, on extraordinary Occasions, convene both houses, or either of them, and in Case of Disagreement between them, with Respect to the Time of Adjournment, he may adjourn them to such Time as he shall think proper; he shall receive Ambassadors and other public Ministers; he shall take Care that the Laws be faithfully executed, and shall Commission all the Officers of the United States.

Section. 4. The President, Vice President and all civil Officers of the United States, shall be removed from Office on Impeachment for, and Conviction of, Treason, Bribery, or other high Crimes and Misdemeanors.

Article III.

Section. 1. The judicial Power of the United States, shall be vested in one supreme Court, and in such inferior Courts as the Congress may from time to time ordain and establish. The Judges, both of the supreme and inferior Courts, shall hold their Offices during good Behaviour, and shall, at stated Times, receive for their Services, a Compensation, which shall not be diminished during their Continuance in Office.

Section. 2. The judicial Power shall extend to all Cases, in Law and equity, arising under this Constitution, the Laws of the United States, and Treaties made, or which shall be made, under their Authority;—to all Cases affecting Ambassadors, other public Ministers and Consuls;—to all Cases of admiralty and maritime Jurisdiction;—to Controversies to which the United States shall be a Party;—to Controversies between two or more States;—[between a State and Citizens of another State;—][8]

---

[8]Changed by the Eleventh Amendment.

between Citizens of different States;— between Citizens of the same State claiming Lands under Grants of different States, [and between a State, or the Citizens thereof, and foreign States, Citizens or Subjects.][9]

In all Cases affecting Ambassadors, other public Ministers and Consuls, and those in which a State shall be Party, the supreme Court shall have original Jurisdiction. In all the other Cases before mentioned, the supreme Court shall have appellate Jurisdiction, both as to Law and Fact, with such exceptions, and under such Regulations as the Congress shall make.

The Trial of all Crimes, except in Cases of Impeachment, shall be by Jury; and such Trial shall be held in the State where the said Crimes shall have been committed; but when not committed within any State, the Trial shall be at such Place or Places as the Congress may by Law have directed.

Section. 3. Treason against the United States, shall consist only in levying War against them, or in adhering to their enemies, giving them Aid and Comfort. No Person shall be convicted of Treason unless on the Testimony of two Witnesses to the same overt Act, or on Confession in open Court.

The Congress shall have Power to declare the Punishment of Treason, but no Attainder of Treason shall work Corruption of Blood, or Forfeiture except during the Life of the Person attainted.

Article. IV.

Section. 1. Full Faith and Credit shall be given in each State to the public Acts, Records, and judicial Proceedings of every other State; And the Congress may by general Laws prescribe the Manner in which such Acts, Records and Proceedings shall be proved, and the effect thereof.

Section. 2. The Citizens of each State shall be entitled to all Privileges and Immunities of Citizens in the several States.

A Person charged in any State with Treason, Felony, or other Crime, who shall flee from Justice, and be found in another State, shall on Demand of the executive Authority of the State from which he fled, be delivered up, to be removed to the State having Jurisdiction of the Crime.

---

[9]Changed by the Eleventh Amendment.

[No Person held to Service or Labour in one State, under the Laws thereof, escaping into another, shall, in Consequence of any Law or Regulation therein, be discharged from such Service or Labour, but shall be delivered up on Claim of the Party to whom such Service or Labour may be due.][10]

Section. 3. New States may be admitted by the Congress into this Union; but no new State shall be formed or erected within the Jurisdiction of any other State; nor any State be formed by the Junction of two or more States, or Parts of States, without the Consent of the Legislatures of the States concerned as well as of the Congress.

The Congress shall have Power to dispose of and make all needful Rules and Regulations respecting the Territory or other Property belonging to the United States; and nothing in this Constitution shall be so construed as to Prejudice any Claims of the United States, or of any particular State.

Section. 4. The United States shall guarantee to every State in this Union a Republican Form of Government, and shall protect each of them against Invasion; and on Application of the Legislature, or of the executive (when the Legislature cannot be convened) against domestic Violence.

Article. V.

The Congress, whenever two thirds of both houses shall deem it necessary, shall propose Amendments to this Constitution, or, on the Application of the Legislatures of two thirds of the several States, shall call a Convention for proposing Amendments, which, in either Case, shall be valid to all Intents and Purposes, as Part of this Constitution, when ratified by the Legislatures of three fourths of the several States, or by Conventions in three fourths thereof, as the one or the other Mode of Ratification may be proposed by the Congress; Provided that no Amendment which may be made prior to the Year One thousand eight hundred and eight shall in any Manner affect the first and fourth Clauses in the Ninth Section of the first Article; and that no State, without its Consent, shall be deprived of it's equal Suffrage in the Senate.

---

[10]Changed by the Thirteenth Amendment.

Article.VI.

All Debts contracted and engagements entered into, before the Adoption of this Constitution, shall be as valid against the United States under this Constitution, as under the Confederation.

This Constitution, and the Laws of the United Signers of the Constitution of the United States of america States which shall be made in Pursuance thereof; and all Treaties made, or which shall be made, under the Authority of the United States, shall be the supreme Law of the Land; and the Judges in every State shall be bound thereby, any Thing in the Constitution or Laws of any State to the Contrary notwithstanding.

The Senators and Representatives before mentioned, and the Members of the several State Legislatures, and all executive and judicial Officers, both of the United States and of the several States, shall be bound by Oath or Affirmation, to support this Constitution; but no religious Test shall ever be required as a Qualification to any Office or public Trust under the United States.

Article.VII.

The Ratification of the Conventions of nine States, shall be sufficient for the Establishment of this Constitution between the States so ratifying the Same.

Done in Convention by the Unanimous Consent of the States present the Seventeenth Day of September in the Year of our Lord one thousand seven hundred and eighty seven and of the Independence of the United States of America the Twelfth In Witness whereof We have hereunto subscribed our Names,

G°.Washington—Presidet and Deputy from Virginia

Signers of the
Constitution of the United States of America

New Hampshire

John Langdon

Nicholas Gilman

Massachusetts

Nathaniel Gorham

Rufus King

Connecticut

Wm. Saml. Johnson

Roger Sherman

New York

Alexander Hamilton

New Jersey

Wil: Livingston

David Brearley

Wm. Paterson

Jona: Dayton

Pennsylvania

B Franklin

Thomas Mifflin

Robt Morris

Geo. Clymer

Thos. FitzSimons

Jared Ingersoll

James Wilson

Gouv Morris

Delaware

Geo: Read

Gunning Bedford jun

John Dickinson

Richard Bassett

Jaco: Broom

Maryland

James McHenry

Dan of St Thos. Jenifer

Danl Carroll

Virginia

John Blair—

James Madison Jr.

North Carolina

Wm. Blount

Richd. Dobbs Spaight

Hu Williamson

South Carolina

J. Rutledge

Charles Cotesworth Pinckney

Charles Pinckney

Pierce Butler

Georgia

William Few

Abr Baldwin

Attest William Jackson Secretary

In Convention Monday
September 17th 1787.

Present
The States of

New hampshire, Massachusetts, Connecticut, Mr. hamilton from NewYork, New Jersey, Pennsylvania, Delaware, Maryland, Virginia, North Carolina, South Carolina and Georgia.

Resolved,

That the preceeding Constitution be laid before the United States in Congress assembled, and that it is the Opinion of this Convention, that it should afterwards be submitted to a Convention of Delegates, chosen in each State by the People thereof, under the Recommendation of its Legislature, for their Assent and Ratification; and that each Convention assenting to, and ratifying the Same, should give Notice thereof to the United States in Congress assembled. Resolved, That it is the Opinion of this Convention, that as soon as the Conventions of nine States shall have ratified this Constitution, the United States in Congress assembled should fix a Day on which Electors should be appointed by the States which shall have ratified the same, and a Day on which the Electors should assemble to vote for the President, and the Time and Place for commencing Proceedings under this Constitution.

That after such Publication the electors should be appointed, and the Senators and Representatives elected: That the electors should meet on the Day fixed for the Election of the President, and should transmit their Votes certified, signed, sealed and directed, as the Constitution requires, to the Secretary of the United States in Congress assembled, that the Senators and Representatives should convene at the Time and Place assigned; that the Senators should appoint a President of the Senate, for the sole Purpose of receiving, opening and counting the Votes for President; and, that after he shall be chosen, the Congress, together with the President, should, without Delay, proceed to execute this Constitution.

By the unanimous Order of the Convention
G°. WAShINGTON—President

W. JACKSON Secretary.

Congress of The United States[11]

begun and held at the City of New-York,
on Wednesday the fourth of March,
one thousand seven hundred and eighty nine

The Conventions of a number of the States, having at the time of their adopting the Constitution, expressed a desire, in order to prevent misconstruction or abuse of its powers, that further declaratory and restrictive clauses should be added: And as extending the ground of public confidence in the Government, will best ensure the beneficent ends of its institution:

ReSOLVeD by the Senate and house of Representatives of the United States of America, in Congress assembled, two thirds of both houses concurring, that the following Articles be proposed to the Legislatures of the several States, as Amendments to the Constitution of the United States, all or any of which Articles, when ratified by three fourths of the said Legislatures, to be valid to all intents and purposes, as part of the said Constitution; viz.t.

ARTICLeS in addition to, and Amendment of the Constitution of the United States of America, proposed by Congress, and ratified by the Legislatures of the several States, pursuant to the fifth Article of the original Constitution....

FReDeRICK AUGUSTUS MUhLeNBeRG
Speaker of the house of Representatives.
JOhN ADAMS, Vice-President of the United States,
and President of the Senate.

ATTEST,
JOhN BeCKLeY, Clerk of the house of Representatives.
SAM. A. OTIS, Secretary of the Senate.

---

[11]On September 25, 1789, Congress transmitted to the state legislatures twelve proposed amendments, two of which, having to do with Congressional representation and Congressional pay, were not adopted. The remaining ten amendments became the Bill of Rights. The amendment concerning Congressional pay was ratified on May 7, 1992, becoming the Twenty-Seventh Amendment to the Constitution.

AMENDMENTS[12]
TO THE CONSTITUTION OF THE
UNITED STATES OF AMERICA

Amendment I.

Congress shall make no law respecting an establishment of religion, or prohibiting the free exercise thereof; or abridging the freedom of speech, or of the press; or the right of the people peaceably to assemble, and to petition the Government for a redress of grievances.

Amendment II.

A well regulated Militia, being necessary to the security of a free State, the right of the people to keep and bear Arms, shall not be infringed.

Amendment III.

No Soldier shall, in time of peace be quartered in any house, without the consent of the Owner, nor in time of war, but in a manner to be prescribed by law.

Amendment IV.

The right of the people to be secure in their persons, houses, papers, and effects, against unreasonable searches and seizures, shall not be violated, and no Warrants shall issue, but upon probable cause, supported by Oath or affirmation, and particularly describing the place to be searched, and the persons or things to be seized.

Amendment V.

No person shall be held to answer for a capital, or otherwise infamous crime, unless on a presentment or indictment of a Grand Jury, except in cases arising in the land or naval forces, or in the Militia, when in actual service in time of War or public danger; nor shall any person be subject for the same offence to be twice put in jeopardy of life or limb; nor shall be compelled in any criminal case to be a witness against himself, nor be

---

[12]The first ten Amendments (the Bill of Rights) were ratified effective December 15, 1791.

deprived of life, liberty, or property, without due process of law; nor shall private property be taken for public use, without just compensation.

Amendment VI.

In all criminal prosecutions, the accused shall enjoy the right to a speedy and public trial, by an impartial jury of the State and district wherein the crime shall have been committed; which district shall have been previously ascertained by law, and to be informed of the nature and cause of the accusation; to be confronted with the witnesses against him; to have compulsory process for obtaining witnesses in his favor, and to have the assistance of counsel for his defence.

Amendment VII.

In Suits at common law, where the value in controversy shall exceed twenty dollars, the right of trial by jury shall be preserved, and no fact tried by a jury, shall be otherwise re-examined in any Court of the United States, than according to the rules of the common law.

Amendment VIII.

Excessive bail shall not be required, nor excessive fines imposed, nor cruel and unusual punishments inflicted.

Amendment IX.

The enumeration in the Constitution of certain rights shall not be construed to deny or disparage others retained by the people.

Amendment X.

The powers not delegated to the United States by the Constitution, nor prohibited by it to the States, are reserved to the States respectively, or to the people.

Amendment XI.[13]

The Judicial power of the United States shall not be construed to extend to any suit in law or equity, commenced or prosecuted against one of the United States by Citizens of another State, or by Citizens or Subjects of any Foreign State.

Amendment XII.[14]

The electors shall meet in their respective states, and vote by ballot for President and Vice- President, one of whom, at least, shall not be an inhabitant of the same state with themselves; they shall name in their ballots the person voted for as President, and in distinct ballots the person voted for as Vice-President, and they shall make distinct lists of all persons voted for as President, and of all persons voted for as Vice-President, and of the number of votes for each, which lists they shall sign and certify, and transmit sealed to the seat of the government of the United States, directed to the President of the Senate;—The President of the Senate shall, in the presence of the Senate and house of Representatives, open all the certificates and the votes shall then be counted;—The person having the greatest number of votes for President, shall be the President, if such number be a majority of the whole number of electors appointed; and if no person have such majority, then from the persons having the highest numbers not exceeding three on the list of those voted for as President, the house of Representatives shall choose immediately, by ballot, the President. But in choosing the President, the votes shall be taken by states, the representation from each state having one vote; a quorum for this purpose shall consist of a member or members from two-thirds of the states, and a majority of all the states shall be necessary to a choice. [And if the house of Representatives shall not choose a President whenever the right of choice shall devolve upon them, before the fourth day of March next following, then the Vice-President shall act as President, as in the case of the death or other constitutional disability of the President—][15] The person having the greatest number of votes as Vice-President, shall be the Vice-President, if such number be a majority of the whole number of electors appointed, and if no person have a majority, then from the two

---

[13]The Eleventh Amendment was ratified February 7, 1795.
[14]The Twelfth Amendment was ratified June 15, 1804.
[15]Superseded by section 3 of the Twentieth Amendment.

highest numbers on the list, the Senate shall choose the Vice-President; a quorum for the purpose shall consist of two-thirds of the whole number of Senators, and a majority of the whole number shall be necessary to a choice. But no person constitutionally ineligible to the office of President shall be eligible to that of Vice-President of the United States.

Amendment XIII.[16]

Section 1. Neither slavery nor involuntary servitude, except as a punishment for crime whereof the party shall have been duly convicted, shall exist within the United States, or any place subject to their jurisdiction.

Section 2. Congress shall have power to enforce this article by appropriate legislation.

Amendment XIV.[17]

Section 1. All persons born or naturalized in the United States and subject to the jurisdiction thereof, are citizens of the United States and of the State wherein they reside. No State shall make or enforce any law which shall abridge the privileges or immunities of citizens of the United States; nor shall any State deprive any person of life, liberty, or property, without due process of law; nor deny to any person within its jurisdiction the equal protection of the laws.

Section 2. Representatives shall be apportioned among the several States according to their respective numbers, counting the whole number of persons in each State, excluding Indians not taxed. But when the right to vote at any election for the choice of electors for President and Vice President of the United States, Representatives in Congress, the Executive and Judicial officers of a State, or the members of the Legislature thereof, is denied to any of the male inhabitants of such State, being twenty-one years of age, and citizens of the United States, or in any way abridged, except for participation in rebellion, or other crime, the basis of representation therein shall be reduced in the proportion which the number of such male citizens shall bear to the whole number of male citizens twenty-one years of age in such State.

---

[16]The Thirteenth Amendment was ratified December 6, 1865.
[17]The Fourteenth Amendment was ratified July 9, 1868.

Section 3. No person shall be a Senator or Representative in Congress, or elector of President and Vice President, or hold any office, civil or military, under the United States, or under any State, who, having previously taken an oath, as a member of Congress, or as an officer of the United States, or as a member of any State legislature, or as an executive or judicial officer of any State, to support the Constitution of the United States, shall have engaged in insurrection or rebellion against the same, or given aid or comfort to the enemies thereof. But Congress may by a vote of two-thirds of each house, remove such disability.

Section 4.The validity of the public debt of the United States, authorized by law, including debts incurred for payment of pensions and bounties for services in suppressing insurrection or rebellion, shall not be questioned. But neither the United States nor any State shall assume or pay any debt or obligation incurred in aid of insurrection or rebellion against the United States, or any claim for the loss or emancipation of any slave; but all such debts, obligations and claims shall be held illegal and void.

Section 5. The Congress shall have power to enforce, by appropriate legislation, the provisions of this article.

Amendment XV.[18]

Section 1. The right of citizens of the United States to vote shall not be denied or abridged by the United States or by any State on account of race, color, or previous condition of servitude.

Section 2. The Congress shall have power to enforce this article by appropriate legislation.

Amendment XVI.[19]

The Congress shall have power to lay and collect taxes on incomes, from whatever source derived, without apportionment among the several States, and without regard to any census or enumeration.

---

[18]The Fifteenth Amendment was ratified February 3, 1870.
[19]The Sixteenth Amendment was ratified February 3, 1913.

Amendment XVII.[20]

The Senate of the United States shall be composed of two Senators from each State, elected by the people thereof, for six years; and each Senator shall have one vote. The electors in each State shall have the qualifications requisite for electors of the most numerous branch of the State legislatures.

When vacancies happen in the representation of any State in the Senate, the executive authority of such State shall issue writs of election to fill such vacancies: Provided, That the legislature of any State may empower the executive thereof to make temporary appointments until the people fill the vacancies by election as the legislature may direct.

This amendment shall not be so construed as to affect the election or term of any Senator chosen before it becomes valid as part of the Constitution.

Amendment XVIII.[21]

[**Section 1**. After one year from the ratification of this article the manufacture, sale, or transportation of intoxicating liquors within, the importation thereof into, or the exportation thereof from the United States and all territory subject to the jurisdiction thereof for beverage purposes is hereby prohibited.

Section 2. The Congress and the several States shall have concurrent power to enforce this article by appropriate legislation.

Section 3. This article shall be inoperative unless it shall have been ratified as an amendment to the Constitution by the legislatures of the several States, as provided in the Constitution, within seven years from the date of the submission hereof to the States by the Congress.]

Amendment XIX.[22]

The right of citizens of the United States to vote shall not be denied or abridged by the United States or by any State on account of sex.

Congress shall have power to enforce this article by appropriate legislation.

---

[20]The Seventeenth Amendment was ratified April 8, 1913.

[21]The Eighteenth Amendment was ratified January 16, 1919.

It was repealed by the Twenty-First Amendment, December 5, 1933.

[22]The Nineteenth Amendment was ratified August 18, 1920.

Amendment XX.[23]

Section 1. The terms of the President and the Vice President shall end at noon on the 20th day of January, and the terms of Senators and Representatives at noon on the 3d day of January, of the years in which such terms would have ended if this article had not been ratified; and the terms of their successors shall then begin.

Section 2. The Congress shall assemble at least once in every year, and such meeting shall begin at noon on the 3d day of January, unless they shall by law appoint a different day.

Section 3. If, at the time fixed for the beginning of the term of the President, the President elect shall have died, the Vice President elect shall become President. If a President shall not have been chosen before the time fixed for the beginning of his term, or if the President elect shall have failed to qualify, then the Vice President elect shall act as President until a President shall have qualified; and the Congress may by law provide for the case wherein neither a President elect nor a Vice President elect shall have qualified, declaring who shall then act as President, or the manner in which one who is to act shall be selected, and such person shall act accordingly until a President or Vice President shall have qualified.

Section 4. The Congress may by law provide for the case of the death of any of the persons from whom the house of Representatives may choose a President whenever the right of choice shall have devolved upon them, and for the case of the death of any of the persons from whom the Senate may choose a Vice President whenever the right of choice shall have devolved upon them.

Section 5. Sections 1 and 2 shall take effect on the 15th day of October following the ratification of this article.

Section 6. This article shall be inoperative unless it shall have been ratified as an amendment to the Constitution by the legislatures of three-fourths of the several States within seven years from the date of its submission.

Amendment XXI.[24]

Section 1.The eighteentharticle of amendment to the Constitution of the United States is hereby repealed.

---

[23]The Twentieth Amendment was ratified January 23, 1933.
[24]The Twenty-First Amendment was ratified December 5, 1933.

Section 2. The transportation or importation into any State, Territory, or Possession of the United States for delivery or use therein of intoxicating liquors, in violation of the laws thereof, is hereby prohibited.

Section 3. This article shall be inoperative unless it shall have been ratified as an amendment to the Constitution by conventions in the several States, as provided in the Constitution, within seven years from the date of the submission hereof to the States by the Congress.

Amendment XXII.[25]

Section 1. No person shall be elected to the office of the President more than twice, and no person who has held the office of President, or acted as President, for more than two years of a term to which some other person was elected President shall be elected to the office of President more than once. But this Article shall not apply to any person holding the office of President when this Article was proposed by the Congress, and shall not prevent any person who may be holding the office of President, or acting as President, during the term within which this Article becomes operative from holding the office of President or acting as President during the remainder of such term.

Section 2. This article shall be inoperative unless it shall have been ratified as an amendment to the Constitution by the legislatures of three-fourths of the several States within seven years from the date of its submission to the States by the Congress.

Amendment XXIII.[26]

Section 1. The District constituting the seat of Government of the United States shall appoint in such manner as Congress may direct:

A number of electors of President and Vice President equal to the whole number of Senators and Representatives in Congress to which the District would be entitled if it were a State, but in no event more than the least populous State; they shall be in addition to those appointed by the States, but they shall be considered, for the purposes of the election of President and Vice President, to be electors appointed by a State; and they shall meet in the District and perform such duties as provided by the twelfth article of amendment.

---

[25]The Twenty-Second Amendment was ratified February 27, 1951.
[26]The Twenty-Third Amendment was ratified March 29, 1961.

Section 2. The Congress shall have power to enforce this article by appropriate legislation.

Amendment XXIV.[27]

Section 1. The right of citizens of the United States to vote in any primary or other election for President or Vice President, for electors for President or Vice President, or for Senator or Representative in Congress, shall not be denied or abridged by the United States or any State by reason of failure to pay any poll tax or other tax.

Section 2. The Congress shall have power to enforce this article by appropriate legislation.

Amendment XXV.[28]

Section 1. In case of the removal of the President from office or of his death or resignation, the Vice President shall become President.

Section 2. Whenever there is a vacancy in the office of the Vice President, the President shall nominate a Vice President who shall take office upon confirmation by a majority vote of both houses of Congress.

Section 3. Whenever the President transmits to the President pro tempore of the Senate and the Speaker of the house of Representatives his written declaration that he is unable to discharge the powers and duties of his office, and until he transmits to them a written declaration to the contrary, such powers and duties shall be discharged by the Vice President as Acting President.

Section 4. Whenever the Vice President and a majority of either the principal officers of the executive departments or of such other body as Congress may by law provide, transmit to the President pro tempore of the Senate and the Speaker of the house of Representatives their written declaration that the President is unable to discharge the powers and duties of his office, the Vice President shall immediately assume the powers and duties of the office as Acting President.

Thereafter, when the President transmits to the President pro tempore of the Senate and the Speaker of the house of Representatives his written declaration that no inability exists, he shall resume the powers and

---

[27]The Twenty-Fourth Amendment was ratified January 23, 1964.

[28]The Twenty-Fifth Amendment was ratified February 10, 1967.

duties of his office unless the Vice President and a majority of either the principal officers of the executive department or of such other body as Congress may by law provide, transmit within four days to the President pro tempore of the Senate and the Speaker of the house of Representatives their written declaration that the President is unable to discharge the powers and duties of his office. Thereupon Congress shall decide the issue, assembling within forty-eight hours for that purpose if not in session. If the Congress, within twenty-one days after receipt of the latter written declaration, or, if Congress is not in session, within twenty-one days after Congress is required to assemble, determines by two-thirds vote of both houses that the President is unable to discharge the powers and duties of his office, the Vice President shall continue to discharge the same as Acting President; otherwise, the President shall resume the powers and duties of his office.

Amendment XXVI.[29]

Section 1. The right of citizens of the United States, who are eighteen years of age or older, to vote shall not be denied or abridged by the United States or by any State on account of age.
Section 2. The Congress shall have power to enforce this article by appropriate legislation.

Amendment XXVII.[30]

No law, varying the compensation for the services of the Senators and Representatives, shall take effect, until an election of Representatives shall have intervened.

---

[29]The Twenty-Sixth Amendment was ratified July 1, 1971.
[30]Congress submitted the text of the Twenty-Seventh Amendment to the States as part of the proposed Bill of Rights on September 25, 1789. The Amendment was not ratified together with the first ten Amendments, which became effective on December 15, 1791. The Twenty- Seventh Amendment was ratified on May 7, 1992, by vote of Michigan.

DATES TO REMEMBER

May 25, 1787: The Constitutional Convention opens with a quorum of seven states in Philadelphia to discuss revising the Articles of Confederation. eventually, all states but Rhode Island are represented.

September 17, 1787: All 12 state delegations approve the Constitution, 39 delegates sign it of the 42 present, and the Convention formally adjourns.

June 21, 1788: The Constitution becomes effective for the ratifying states when New hampshire is the ninth state to ratify it.

March 4, 1789: The first Congress under the Constitution convenes in New York City.

April 30, 1789: George Washington is inaugurated as the first President of the United States.

June 8, 1789: James Madison introduces the proposed Bill of Rights in the house of Representatives.

September 24, 1789: Congress establishes a Supreme Court, 13 district courts, three ad hoc circuit courts, and the position of Attorney General.

September 25, 1789: Congress approves 12 amendments and sends them to the states for ratification.

February 2, 1790: The Supreme Court convenes for the first time.

December 15, 1791: Virginia ratifies the Bill of Rights, and 10 of the 12 proposed amendments become part of the U.S. Constitution.

"No free government, nor the blessings of liberty, can be preserved to any people, but by...a frequent recurrence to fundamental principles."
— *George Mason, 1776*

"The people made the Constitution, and the people can unmake it. It is the creature of their own will, and lives only by their will."
— *John Marshall, 1821*

"The happy Union of these States is a wonder; their Constitution a miracle; their example the hope of Liberty throughout the world."
— *James Madison, 1829*

"East Avenue School, 1960"

(Barnes & Noble display)
"You won't see this display,
living under a dictatorship."

(Swastica) "Odd, what our
Constitution will allow, huh?"

" Sophie Scholl "

"The Great Seal, reverse"

"The Great Seal" (obverse)

13.

Y ou may remember my reference to the possibility of a nuclear holocaust. Let's revisit that concept for a few more minutes, but dig a little deeper, this time into the waste that bomb making creates, and where it goes. Nuclear waste that continues to pollute our planet, as I write and as you read. The news, however, isn't all bad. In point of fact, there's great news on the horizon.

By 'nuclear waste' I mean waste that's contaminated by plutonium, from the building of the atom bomb. This can include clothing worn by nuclear workers, contaminated dirt or equipment, and waste from making the 1945 atom bomb as well as waste from future nuclear weapons production. Add to that, thirty four + tons of 'surplus plutonium' waste, and we've got a problem.

The problem? Nuclear waste must eventually be disposed somewhere – permanently removed from our environment. It can't just be stored indefinitely or thrown away like regular industrial trash. Radioactive waste must be permanently disposed, far away from the 'accessible' environment in a safe place, where it can cause harm to no one. Such a place, or so thought the government, is in the State of New Mexico, with its deserts and wide open prairie land.

Since the 1940s, New Mexico has been the only state, out of fifty, that allows such permanent disposal of military-generated, plutonium-contaminated waste, Perhaps this is because Los Alamos National Laboratory (LANL), where 'The Bomb' was first created, is in the same state. Granted, most of the waste is being disposed deep below the ground surface. However, the fact remains that the citizenry of only one state is saddled with the responsibility of finding a safe place to dispose all our nation's atom bomb-making waste. The betrayal is greater because New Mexico was promised that WIPP would be a pilot project for other repositories in other states that would share the responsibility.

This disposal takes place 2150 feet below the ground surface at the Waste Isolation Pilot Plant (WIPP), a state and federal repository for plutonium-contaminated waste near the city of Carlsbad, New Mexico. This is the first and only, deep geological disposal facility for radioactive waste in the world. Enter the Stop Forever WIPP Coalition (StopForeverWIPP.org), a coalition of environmental and antinuke groups throughout New Mexico that are fighting the Department of Energy's (DOE) current plans to expand WIPP. Created a few years ago to address WIPP's intention to more than double in size and to stay open forever (thus, "Forever" WIPP.) Some groups in the coalition have been around since the 1970s. Because DOE is also "expanding" LANL, which itself, has been here since the 1940s, and because this new work will generate new waste for WIPP, Stop Forever WIPP is also attempting to rein in the waste forged by LANL.

Hundreds, maybe thousands of other movements, dedicated only to the end of things that are harmful to the human race exist, some that have been mentioned here. However, the Stop Forever WIPP Coalition deserves special attention because those within the campaign have stuck to it for so long. I have a friend who's been fighting WIPP for over forty years. When anyone stays with a campaign for more than ten years, you can be sure it's something for which attention of the populous is long overdue, even if it's for only one state. And why not?

Should the nuclear waste ever find its way to the rivers, the ground, the atmosphere, everything, including the air we breathe, would be contaminated for about as long as the universe has existed. Literally. It will take that long for all the plutonium to turn into something 'safe.' Nothing will grow, the air and clouds, like the ground, will be poisoned, as will the water we drink, if any. Newer and better ways for the human race to kill itself off? You betcha!

But help is on the way. The DOE has mandated that no fewer than thirty 'pits' or triggers for nuclear weapons, per year – every year – be manufactured at LANL. The most LANL has been able to build in the past was eleven triggers over several years, and they contaminated the plutonium building doing that, shutting it down for years. Stop Forever WIPP, despite DOE's intentions, has stepped in, with radio, newspaper and online ads, petitions, and brochures that explain, for the complete idiot, what the DOE is up to, at both WIPP and LANL. It's a start, yes? Of course, a better start would be a nearperfect world, in which there's no such thing as plutonium and nuclear bombs.

14.

I n other parts of the globe, though confined to these United States, nineteen states' Attorneys General have put their respective Governors on notice, that they'll be having a look at your medical records, for any old reason. While this includes men, particular emphasis is placed on pregnant women, who seek out of state abortions. In other parts of the country, fascists -- the ones who were elected in free and fair elections – are up to their old tricks in Alabama and Ohio. And they really are tricks. But, as promised, we'll make the details of those tricks a part of our closing statement. Yours and mine.

Fascism is coast to coast. Perhaps you believe that if you see no swastika, it doesn't exist. No, they've traded in their swastikas for suits and ties. Makes them harder to spot, especially with the perpetual smile, although if you see an "R" next to their name, it's a fairly safe bet that he's a fascist. Hypocrisy is their cornerstone. Lying is but a tool in their box of many tricks. Balanced people see right through the lies. There's a book entitled "The Dumbing Down Of America," by Robert Hetrick and Julie Hetrick, which your author avidly recommends reading.

A few words about the separation of church and state, also found in this nation's Constitution. The mistakes from which our Founding Fathers had hoped to learn, were made by their own founders, in their respective native lands. The difference being, their founders were all fascists, and the immortalized document known as this country's Constitution, is based solely on the democracy in which we, in the USA, are alleged to have been a part. You know the one. It gives you the right to say anything, publicly, short of screaming "fire!" in a crowded theater.

The separation was going well until 1957, when the "Red Scare" caused a mass paranoia to set in among the lawmakers. Seems the concepts of communism and socialism were so closely interchangeable, or so believed our lawmakers at the time, that they went ahead and changed the wording on all Silver Certificates (paper money), from "E Pluribus Unum" (out of many, one) to "In God We Trust," so as to not allow adversaries and non-adversaries alike to even think that the USA had somehow turned communist. Overnight. But E pluribus unum wasn't only printed on paper money. It had been the De Facto motto of the United States since 1782, when the Congress enacted it to, among other things, be inscribed on the Great Seal, where the motto remains to this day.

There's also the little matter of the "Pledge of Allegiance" to the flag. Written by Francis Bellamy in 1892, the 'Pledge' went out of its way not to make mention of God or religion. However, also during the Red Scare, the U.S. Congress inserted the words "Under God" to the pledge in 1954.

This, in the event that you hadn't noticed, is all about fear. Fear of communism, fear of socialism, and fear of your fellow man or woman. That panic is resurfacing in 2024, with the same old, dredged up fears, but all dressed up to appear differently, though the rational adult knows better. Do you fear the evolution of women, from helpless female, capable only of screaming, cooking and having babies, to becoming capable of doing work or jobs once thought of as "men's work"? Do you fear science and medical evolution? The educated man or woman?

It's true that in chapters past, I complained about the human race's inability to compete with, or keep up with technology, but that complaint does not extend to social evolution. Let's get back to those fears. First up, communism. The line between communism and socialism, thanks to people who call themselves leaders, is apparently forever blurred. Please allow your humble host to add some clarity. We've discussed socialism, and how it's working for America, to some extent, and to discuss it further would only belabor the point.

That said, let's discuss communism. Its concept is thousands of years old, and to be successful, almost always requires a dictator. This, because it's assumed that the 'masses' know little or nothing about how to become educated individuals and live their singular lives. Certain fascist politicians right here in the USA have floated that concept, though, thankfully, were not completely successful. Everything, from media to the food on your table, is sponsored by the government. And that's how the government prefers it. No government, no food. It's as simple as that. Those who believe that communism and socialism are somehow connected are dead wrong. Not to be outdone, Willful ignorance remains an integral part of the mix. There continues to stubbornly exist those who, for whatever reason, don't want to believe or know the truth.

15.

The time has come to address voter suppression in Alabama and Ohio. Not that it doesn't exist elsewhere in the Republic, but for now, we'll focus our attentions on these two states. In defiance of a Supreme Court order, the legislature of the State of Alabama has sent a resounding NO to the remainder of the country, with regard to the gerrymandering of that state's many voting districts. While I won't get into the specifics of the SCOTUS order, it's safe to say that the state's Governor did not get the decision for which he'd hoped. For any who may not know, to 'gerrymander' is to manipulate the boundaries of an electoral constituency, so as to favor one party or class.

The state of Alabama is 26% Black, but, due to heavily gerrymandered districting, has only one congressman of color. The SCOTUS handed down a 6/3 decision, the essence of which said that the state needs to draw new and fairer district boundary lines, to which the Alabama politicians, all white, and all elected, compliments of the gerrymandered districts, have responded in the negative. In other words, they told the highest court in the land to go screw itself. Funny how, when the High Court reversed Roe vs. Wade, thereby taking away fifty years of freedom of choice, not to mention the doctor/patient confidentiality for women, they were all for it. But where race is concerned, they can't be manipulated by an institution, some 2,000 miles away.

Meanwhile, in the state of Ohio, the news is much better. Seems they held a "special election," regarding a state Constitutional Amendment, that would protect a woman's right to choose. At first, politicians who call themselves conservatives, thought that having an 'off year' election was a great idea. People wouldn't vote, or perhaps would forget to vote. And, as I'm sure you're aware, when people don't vote, the conservative element wins, every time. Fascists went out of their way to keep it an off year election, with just that in mind. Not this time, however. Those who wanted the right to amend the state's Constitution, to ensure a woman's right to choose, won overwhelmingly. Firstly, the conservative element attempted to raise the percentage of approval from voters, from fifty to sixty percent. They knew full well the intention of the minority in the state's House was to introduce legislation that would guarantee a woman's right to choose. When the 50 to 60 percent approval of voters went down in flames in the first 'special election', the conservative element went back to the drawing board and came up with the purging of 26,000 registered voters from legitimate voter rolls. Didn't work. The voters came back anyway, and approved an abortion guarantee for any woman who wants it. See what happens when people get out and vote? Hopefully, all those voters will be back for the 2024 election.

That's just the tip of the proverbial iceberg. It proved what Americans can do when they vote in large numbers. The trick, you see, is to get Americans to vote in large numbers in every election, because, like cockroaches, fascists will take over if they get so much as slender thread of an opening. And, as I've stressed, once in, they're like flypaper, sticky as hell and impossible to be rid of forever. The answer to this and other quandaries is not fear. It is, again, logic and common sense. Don't forget to vote!

Also, and I can't say this enough, so please bare with me, it's unfortunate that we, as Americans, must choose a side. Actually, there's good news on that front, too. Seems that 85% of Americans have come together over a woman's right to choose. Makes sense. Would you rather a politician or your private physician helps you to make what could be the most important decision of your life? The politician's way is cruelty and control. Kids can be cruel to one another, but they have a legitimate excuse. They haven't had time to learn compassion. Fascism, on the other hand, is cruelty with an adult agenda.

A few words now, about groups of people who've come together to help with the fight for human rights. Here in the USA, some, like the American Civil Liberties Union (ACLU), can afford to pay workers for their duties, but most are like my friend in New Mexico. They are volunteers. This because they believe in what they are doing. Around the world, people fight fascism because they have no choice. In places like Ukraine, where the Russian Army has mercilessly bombed hospitals and day care centers, in an unprovoked effort to give more power to only one person, it's a fight or die situation. Places like Israel, where anti-fascists have taken to the streets by the hundreds of thousands, to protest their Prime Minister, who's under indictment, by the by, for his willingness to change the laws, so as for him to not be under indictment. In Russia, where a fascist dictator, with the help of his military, has managed to cower an entire populous and turn them into sheep, while threatening same with fine or imprisonment, should they so much as take part in a peaceful protest. Yes, there remain the brave ones, who risk imprisonment, because they believe that they have no choice. And those brave ones will be remembered by history as patriots, like myself, who remained and stood up to the dictators who dared to rule a single land, just because they believed they could.

I don't pretend to know a lot about the Black or Native People's experience in America. But thanks to Miss Smith and books that have long since been banned, I know enough to know that they are people with heartbeats, deserving a crack at "the good life;" and that what is happening on their behalf is not at all what the Founding Fathers had in mind when they threw together the Constitution. If your belief is anything else, here's your hat.

I'm just one man, and an author at that. A nobody. As such, I don't expect to change any minds. Perhaps help to make a few folks think things over, is all I ask. I can't say that I understand the MAGA mentality either. To throw away an experiment that, by most accounts, has been a success, and replace that democracy with a dictatorship – one man, who'll tear down everything that's been built -- is just not logical.

My story about going back to the elementary school where it all began had a purpose. For anyone who may not have understood the first explanation, it was to demonstrate respect and admiration for the office of the Presidency. But, in the case of the forty fifth President, how does one respect a cheater? A liar? A con man? A flimflam man, who hornswoggled his way through college, then the Selective Service System? At least your host stood up to them, and said "No!"

The older members of our reading audience may remember the name Pat Paulson. He was a stand-up comic in the 1960s. His 'shtick' was to run for the Presidency every four years. Younger readers may want to google the name. He was quite funny in his own right. He'd talk of issues that the real candidates dared not touch, like burgeoning homelessness, the consistently devalued dollar and the stagnant growth of available jobs in the 60s.

When the eventual winner of the 2016 race for the Presidency first came down his gold plated escalator, I honestly believed he was "Pulling a Pat," and that there'd be no way rational adults would ever vote for him. Silly me. I went on to endure four years of lies. About 30,000 of them. He threw paper towels at people in the Philippines, when he should have been offering monetary assistance, used his own Sharpie pen to change the direction of a hurricane, so that he'd be right. The only legislation he was able to pass successfully was a higher tax rate for the rich. As a result of his taking office, he's been indicted four times, the third for inciting an insurrection, as a sore loser. In all, he's accrued ninety one felonies. And you want him back? In good faith, I have to state that I really don't get it. Jim Jones would be proud. More about him later.

About every 270 years, another democracy falls into a dictatorship. It's happened in Nigeria, Nepal, Indonesia and Russia (the USSR). Does the line of declining democracies lead to the USA? The peaceful transition of power is no more; fascist politicians in many states have seen fit to make it a near impossibility just to cast a vote; violation of individual rights and the freedom of expression, as guaranteed in the Constitution, have become a past glory, at best. Is it time to tear up that Constitution and the Declaration of Independence, in favor of a one-man dictatorship? Study your history. You'll find that the Founding Fathers were right.

It's not too late. Now you too can Learn about the advanced technology, that which Tom Edison was so afraid. More and more, colleges are opening their doors to students who once were monetarily or educationally barred. Doors you won't find opening in any dictatorship. They prefer that their 'subjects' be uneducated, and therefore easier to control.

Getting back to our own education, along came COVID 19. Home study became the norm. Next thing you know, colleges began throwing open their doors to poorer students, but students just the same. Students with a hunger for knowledge, as opposed to a dictator's rants about "his" country. Only he and he alone can make it make it better, or, in the words of someone we all know and love – the same way one might love a two year-old, who's acting out – "fix it." The genius has spoken. Just ask him.

Dictators are traditionally uneducated. If they cheated their way through college, it's the same difference. They constantly accuse others of crimes to which, history shows that they, themselves, are guilty. A sort of reverse narcissism. But then there's really nothing 'reverse' about it. Just a matter of who committed the evil first, and who'll take the credit. Count on the dictator.

Narcissis gazed at his own reflection in the water. Hence, we get Narcissism. The rules have been stretched a might, to conform with amateur and professional psychiatric profundities, but rest assured, that's what he did. Little did he know that someday his namesake would be used to describe a fascist politician.

16.

A simple way to see the optimist/pessimist argument is the half full glass vs. the half empty glass. A deeper way to look at the subject might be that the optimist will build something – anything – out of little or nothing, while the evil one will simply burn it all down in order to rule over the ashes (Sun Tzu).

I spoke briefly about my country's own Civil War in previous chapters. Now, if you please, a bit more depth. Anyone who's been in actual bloody combat will be the first to argue against it. From infantrymen, all the way to the President (Eisenhower), they've seen, up close and personal, the horrors of war, and want no part of it.

The American Civil War is, to date, the bloodiest of all war efforts, world wide. Beginning at Fort Sumter, and ending at the Appomattox Courthouse, the conflict lasted just under four years, but during that short four years, managed to take 620,000 American lives. 620,000 hearts, most of them young, stopped beating. The average age of a soldier was twenty five. Americans fought against one another, sometimes brothers from the same family, on behalf of eleven Southern states, whose Constitutionally constructed legislatures decided that they didn't like the way President Lincoln did things. Although the freedom of slaves was a paramount issue, it wasn't the only issue.

Fascists, from street showoff to well-dressed politician, calling for another Civil War, have never actually been in combat. They've never seen a sucking chest wound that shoots out blood with every breath; never seen an actual compound fracture, where the bloodied bone is exposed; never seen a soldier gasp for breath, then die in their arms. In June of 1879, William Tecumseh Sherman, in a speech to the graduating class of the Michigan Military Academy, proclaimed "I am tired and sick of war. Its glory is all moonshine. It is only those who have neither fired a shot, nor heard the shrieks and groans of the wounded, who cry aloud for blood, for vengeance, for desolation. War is hell." And regardless of his past, on the subject of war, he knew whereof he spoke.

The so-called 'sanctuary cities,' to which the South has sent numerous busloads of immigrants, is an idea that many Southern politicians think is original. However, in 1961, around the peak of the Civil Rights movement, throngs of Black people were loaded into busses like cattle and, with little or no knowledge of their destination, bussed North. They were told that jobs, wealth and comfortable housing awaited them, when the reality was no job, no wealth, and certainly no housing, comfortable or otherwise. It was sort of a "neener-neener" move by Southern politicians to their counterparts in the North. That is, until the money ran out.

Meanwhile, the unwitting human beings were welcomed with open arms in the North. The plan, for the most part, had backfired. And by now, the funds had dried up. They, being just like you, perhaps reading this, were, and continue to be Americans. The funding, however, for today's version of the 'reverse freedom rides' is unlimited, of course at our own taxpayer expense, and the immigrants continue to be welcomed, in whichever Northern city or town they happen to land.

On the subject of immigrants, we'll need to cover the ongoing conflict in Ukraine, and yet another example of American political hypocrisy. Seems the self-styled conservatives have found a new punching bag, and Ukraine is its name. They don't believe that American support for the Ukrainian fight against fascism, both morally and monetarily, with a few tanks and other armaments thrown in for good measures, is justified, and that our tax dollars would be better spent on the bussing of immigrants to sanctuary cities.

Students of history, American or otherwise, will know at a glance that the Ukrainian disagreement, replete with shrewd undertones on both sides of the aisle, is not the first time politicians have traveled this road. That we're aware of, it's the second.

In 1935, Italy, with Mussolini at the helm, made the arbitrary decision to invade and otherwise conquer a small, inconspicuous country in Africa, known as Ethiopia. Africa had only two neutral countries at the time. Ethiopia was one of them. Still reeling from WWI, the balance of Europe was reticent to jump into yet another military conflict. But American fascism was alive and well, and ready to fall in behind Mussolini. Recruiters stood literally on street corners, ready to sign the most unsuspecting, youthful, white, American Son, who hungered for, but had not yet seen the actual horrors of war. American politics were mostly neutral concerning the potential conflict, having had a hand, in no small way, in WWI. The League of Nations, which would fold in April of 1946, after being unable to prevent what eventually became WWII, stepped in, but was unable to stop Italy's aggression, and Ethiopia, following the bloody attack of men, women and children, became another Italian colony. In 1941, the British Empire, with assistance from Ethiopian Arbegnoch Guerillas, sent Italy packing, never to return to Ethiopia.

It's important to note the similarities that existed between the Italian and Russian invasions. Both attacks were ordered by a crazed dictator, with an unquenchable thirst for power. Both attacks were wholly unprovoked. Both attacks involved the slaughter of unsuspecting men, women and children, sometimes even babies. That, nonetheless, is where the similarities end.

Ukraine didn't turn out to be the pushover that Vladimir Putan had assumed, when he ordered the troops to invade. They were met with resistance on a grand scale. For every dictatorship that arises, there's a democracy waiting to meet it. Choose your side carefully, as there's no turning back. Your author's convinced that if 80% of Russia's citizens had their way, they'd be living in a democracy. On the subject of democracies, it looks as though ours, here in the USA, is under attack. Had to happen. People get bored with success. Bored with low joblessness. Bored with the numerous successes of an administration that managed to put money directly into the hands of the citizenry, regardless of political persuasion, your host, who's not a rich man, having been one of them.

The American President was able, through the Inflation Reduction Act, to send $350 Million to the state of Florida, earmarked to weatherize household appliances. The Governor immediately turned it down, saying it's "just another attempt at woke," or words to that effect. Two months later, Hurricane Idalia flooded the state. Having turned down the $350 million, the State of Florida no longer qualifies for, and could not access $341 million, allotted to fund the state's own energy conservation program.

Florida's Governor wasn't finished. He, also two months prior to Idalia, rejected an additional $3 million, to help fight pollution, and to help fund the "Solar For All" program, a nonprofit, which helps low-income people obtain solar panels. The Inflation Reduction Act (IRA) contains the most sweeping climate change components in U.S. History.

As a peripheral to the Governor's turn-down of any part of the IRA, insurance companies are leaving Florida, by the flock. They quite simply, can no longer afford to cover Floridians, and still make a profit. In the insurance industry, it is an unfortunate fact of life that it's all about profit.

The Federal Emergency Management Act or FEMA has stepped in to assist homeowners with issues arising out of the mass flooding. Governor Desantis seems quiet about that. Careful, Gov, there may be a few Democrats, skulking, waiting to take away your freedoms and, you know, all of the other things you accuse them of taking away, that you, yourself are guilty.

17.

S ince the Voting Rights Act of 1965 was gutted by a recent Supreme Court decision, in the state of Wisconsin, a peculiar situation exists. Seems their Governor, Lt. Governor and Secretary of State are all Democrats. Almost everyone else, politically speaking, is a Republican. Could the reason be that in a general election, everybody votes, regardless of how gerrymandered lines are drawn? Political gerrymandering is bad in Wisconsin. So much so, that a Democrat can win an election, by a decisive margin, but the Republican opponent will legally take office. To explain how that happens would be confusing, to say the least, convoluted, to say the most. Besides, the practice of gerrymandering is defined in a recent chapter.

The Supreme Court weighed in, saying Wisconsin's over-gerrymandered maps very obviously discriminated against Black voters, but the Wisconsin State House, like Alabama, has chosen to ignore that particular decision. Is it something in the air, that turns rational adults into aimless fascists? Or a certain brand of Kool-Aid, perhaps?

In addition to the gerrymandering mess, the state of Wisconsin recently held a special election, for a State Supreme Court Justice, which was won overwhelmingly, at 11%, by the liberal challenger. Caught off guard by her win, which gave the State Court a Democratic majority, self-styled conservatives had a plan 'B'. Put simply, the plan 'B' was to impeach her, without a trial, and with no allegations of misconduct. But then, how could there be? The Justice-elect had yet to hear her first case. The plan, at any rate, would seem to be going well, save for the fact that the Wisconsin Governor is a Democrat. Thus, the chances are little to none that the self-styled conservatives will have their way. Quite a safety net, huh? Again, most unfortunate that all must choose a side. Was a time when D's and R's could work out their differences by putting their heads together, sometimes literally, and working out a compromise. But back then, fascism was not the least bit involved in the outcome. They were all adults. How many American Senators and Congress People can say that, in the present day? Unfortunately, very few. Incidentally, the grounds under which the new Justice will be impeached are the very grounds on which she ran her successful campaign, to save democracy. In the meantime, they've hatched a scheme whereby anyone who assists a pregnant woman to a state that allows abortion, will suffer the wrath of the law. What that means is if you need a ride to California, and if I give you that ride, I could be arrested. Guess they better catch me before I get out of the state.

Meanwhile, in Texas – where else? – the Wilkes Brothers, all two of them, have seen to it that school age children can now watch videos about how renewable energy is just a 'woke' hoax, designed, like every other woke hoax, to mislead children into believing that there really is no climate change. The Wilkes Brothers have spent upwards from three million dollars on this project. Look for the Wilkes name to be much more popular in so-called conservative circles. The Wilkes Brothers can now declare their project a success, as many Texas school boards have approved the videos for release, so that little children can watch our country become an autocracy, while believing it's a "good thing."

It really is like a cancer. But only the super rich seem to get it. Then, they cure it by donating millions of their dollars to the political campaigns of idiots. Here's an example: The Department of Health recently put out a statement that encouraged the consumption, by adults, of two beers per day. Not to be outdone, Ted Cruz, the Senator from Texas, who calls himself a conservative, and whose family originally immigrated from Cuba, immediately pulled a film crew together to encourage the consumption of more than two bottles a day. This, in defiance of the current Administration, that he assumed was only allowing two beers a day, which, of course, is far from the truth. He can read. He knows better, but like you, he chose a side. And now, win or lose, he's stuck with it. You, conversely, are not. You, the reader, can simply walk away. Or can you? Did you buy a gun? Do you intend to use it? Perhaps there's a child, who, in your opinion, needs killing.

Moving to Alabama now, figuratively, of course. Looks as though one Senator has singlehandedly held back 270 military promotions. You may remember the Senator from chapters past, as the man who called, publicly, for shooters to take to the streets. He's held back these promotions for six months. Nominated military positions, from General to Flag Officer can not take their newly promoted place. His complaint?

Seems the four branches of the military have had the audacity to pay leave for pregnant women to either have their babies or abort them. It's fair, but not to the Senator. He, being a Republican, doesn't approve of a woman's right to choose. After all, she might be traveling to one of those liberal states that kills babies. We can't have that. Better that politicians and lawyers should make that decision for her, as opposed to, you know, herself or her doctor, or maybe both. To that end, the Senator has blocked all military promotions that he's able to block. A sort of unexpected perk, for those who call themselves conservative, is that hostile foreign powers, like Russia, are starting to take notice. With so much discord within our own military, how can we be expected to contribute to the win of a conflict such as, oh, Ukraine?

Politicizing is a favorite topic of fascists. As we've discussed, the fascist accuses other 'side' of committing evil deeds, while they, themselves are the guilty ones. Narcissism rears its ugly head, yet again. All of the above is no exception.

18.

A s mentioned earlier, the fascist is generally uneducated. If s/he were more educated, they probably wouldn't be fascist. What wasn't mentioned is how you, the reader, can be smarter than the average fascist. Put simply, *educate and vote*. Or, you can do what I did. All by myself, with a high school education and a little college, I figured out that logic and common sense are the only two ways to happiness, such as it is. But it's not for everyone. It requires deduction, and there's no time for that. Whatever works, right?

Getting back to education, since the advent of COVID, colleges and universities have relaxed their admissions policies. With the college drop-out rate at an all time high, schools are not yet desperate to fill seats, but rapidly approaching that plateau. One might call it a silver lining, if, with over a million American deaths from the COVID 19 virus, that's possible.

A two year college or trade school is the answer for just about anyone. The trades are, as said, many times over, the backbone of our country. If I, personally, had it to do again, it'd be a toss-up between slot machine mechanic and court reporting college, both of which have schools for instruction, again, for the complete idiot, and one for which, your host was a dropout. Neither industry has a whole lot of glamour attached, but the money's outstanding.

Let's have a look at what these two trades have in common. Both require only a high school diploma. If, perchance, you don't have that, there are easy ways to obtain it, not the least of which is usually online. Then, all you have to do is learn how to use a computer, which is supplied. A tall order for some, myself included, though doable. But it's all moot, as, without a high school diploma, I doubt you'll even be reading this. Both trades are 'inflation proof,' meaning, if there's a great, country wide recession, you can still get work, anywhere in the nation, because both trades are always in demand. This is also true of the nursing profession. While I couldn't say what the starting pay is for either trade, I can tell you that, both trades, being as in demand as they are, job security is a given, and where there's job security, good money often follows.

With today's trade schools, you can become anything, from police officer to bus driver to baker. Some schools will even loan you the money to get started in a small business. There is virtually no reason to become a dropout. Unless, of course, that particular lifestyle appeals to you. Your host tried it once. Just once. Didn't like it. Got a job. They say you get used to the panhandling, but I never did. Never got used to sleeping in filth, on 86th Avenue. Never got used to shouting "Right on!" to an amplified voice, the exact words to which escaped me, the moment they were shouted. But, having experienced 'demonstration burnout', I'd heard it all before, at hundreds of constitutionally protected rallies. While I continue to believe in the concepts, after fifty years, fascism has presented us with a whole new set of circumstances.

Where are those amplified voices now? Where are all the protesters? Did they get jobs and raise families? Do they not understand that they can continue on with their jobs and still protest? Why? Because fascism is a very real conviction. It's been around for thousands of years, and now it's nipping at our heels, right here in the USA. The 'opposition' would say, if asked, that they're doing something about it. Let's see, there's 'The Proud Boys'. But they're all terrorists. Ever wonder how you get to be a domestic terrorist? It's fairly simple. There are four factors involved in becoming a domestic terrorist. First, you must be easily manipulated. Second, you must believe all conspiracy theories, regardless of their outlandishness. My favorite? The one about the (dead) Kennedy's coming back from the dead to vote and run for office in the next election, and naturally, regardless of their past, they'll be voting for the fascist. Third, you must be willing to die for the cause. You're no domestic terrorist, unless you're willing to die for the cause.

On another 'up' note, a few words more about scholarships. There are thousands of them, offered by schools, employers, individuals, private companies, nonprofits, communities, religious groups, and professional and social organizations. You may not be going to a 'name' school, but if it's accredited and the diploma's good, who cares?

Racially speaking, the chances of a white student getting a scholarship are 14.2%, while the odds for minority students are 11.2%. The odds of a Black student winning one are 11.4%, 9.1% for Hispanic students, and 10.5% for Asian students. From ThinkImpact (.com)

The leader of the scholarship fund is COCA-COLA, an achievement based scholarship, at $20,000 per year. The award is offered to high school seniors; financial need is not a factor; the deadline month is October. At number two, we have BURGER KING, with a $25,000 fund. Students must demonstrate financial need; deadline month is January. The makers of TIDE have gotten into the act, having donated $1.5 million to a scholarship fund. No word on financial need. From the Edvisors Network.

19.

The President of Poland is Andrzej Duda. Much like in our own USA's 2016 election, he was elected by running a campaign of nothingness. No master plan, no resolutions for his Congress to kick around, and no budget for the next fiscal year. He just bitched about everything. And now, also like our USA, they're stuck with him. In one way or another, mostly free media attention because of his popularity, he'll worm his dictatorial way back into the lives of the unsuspecting electorate.

Much like Israel's Prime Minister, Andrzej has figured out a way around the legal system, so that he can remain clean as a whistle. This is usually done by outlawing all the positions that might otherwise prosecute him. Dictators in 'banana republics' can do that. Fact is, they can do pretty much anything they've a mind to do. Their followers don't just vote for them. They're cultists, and proud of it. It's like they're in a hypnotic trance. They believe anything that comes out of his mouth, as once stated, regardless of its outlandishness.

The American President at the time, took it upon himself to reroute Air Force One, for an unscheduled stop in Poland. He undoubtedly wanted to pick up a few pointers. Or maybe visa-versa. Anything for a fellow dictator.

It appears we didn't learn our lesson(s) of four years ago, as the same wannabe dictator, who was the forty fifth President, is making another run for the Oval Office. It's been proven by psychiatric professionals that he has the mind of a schoolyard bully. He must be watched like a two year-old, lest he walks off with a 'top secret' document. Or two or three or four. And all because he says the documents are "His." Senility is not a factor. Irreversible insanity is. To describe the four years he spent in office might become redundant, as most people around the world are aware of his shenanigans, all designed to make the rich, like himself, richer. It is, to say the very least, flabbergasting to your host, that a major American political party, of which there are only two, has unswervingly endorsed him to run for the highest office in the land *again*. Never mind that, while in office, he lost the Senate, lost the House and yes, despite what his supporters, from behind prison walls say, he lost the Presidency, fair and square. Within the Party, he, however, is the runaway favorite.

It's not my intention to tell you, the reader, how to vote, however, could you please find it in your heart to just vote like a rational adult? You'll be voting for the leader of the free world, and that's no small issue. The eighty million of you that didn't bother to vote in the 2023 and other elections, can now take heart. You have a clean slate, except in Oho, where 43,000 of you seem to be missing, compliments of your local registrar of voters, so try to be ever so vigilant. Before placing the X in the box, do a little homework. This is a big decision, that people fought and died for your right to make. Research your potential candidate. How's his/her voting record, if any? What, if any, promises does either candidate make? Are the promises attainable? He or she will be your President. The same can be said of your Congressional or Senatorial candidate, and while he or she may be more reachable, your President is the Commander in Chief, not of his military, but of *your* military. Regardless of what he may say, the military belongs to you. They fight, when called upon to do so, for you, and to preserve *your* democracy.

Another word to use for the Presidency is experience. You can't suddenly wake up and decide you're going to be the leader of the free world, and expect to be elected. One man did it, and look at the mess he's made. He's laughed at constantly by foreign dignitaries; he's never taken seriously by the electorate (and that works both ways); he throws words around, like "treason" and "disgrace," without ever knowing the words' full meaning; and the world takes notice at what we did, as Americans, when we voted him into office. You may not have voted for him, though, as stated, he won the Electoral College. What was not stated is that he soundly lost the popular vote. The vote that you, the reader, braved foul and fair weather to cast.

After having left office, following in an election which he naturally challenged – and lost, in fifty nine of sixty courtrooms – he was called upon by the National Archives to please return the documents, some marked "Top Secret," with which he absconded, happily on his way to Mar-a-Lago. After returning a few, then swearing there were no more documents to be had, he was subpoenaed. The government had to rent trucks to carry out all the documents that our former President swore he didn't have. You see, while in office, as stated, he told over 30,000 lies. So what's another little blatant lie, among friends?

Legislatively, while in the office he had no business occupying, he was an even bigger joke. Unless you happen to be a billionaire. Only 2% of us are even millionaires, and your guide is most assuredly not one of them. Who needs all that money? To make a living, and have a few dollars left over for fun or children is all fine and well, but billions? There are only 756 billionaires in USA, and they only reside in 42 of our 50 states. Then we have to come up with new and different ways to 'shelter' our billions. Hundreds have done just that, successfully. Dodging the lawsuits successfully, and watching their dollars has become, for many, yet another full time job. And yes, there will be lawsuits. Billionaires should count on that. It comes with the territory.

Civilization is not inherent. Like most things academic, it has to be learned. Everything, from sidewalks to manicured lawns are the direct result of a civilized society in which we thrive. Occasionally, there are those who, due to mental illness or a serious lack of education, do not fit into a society, as we know it. Jails are full of them. I believe it's called "anti-social behavior." While I can't pretend to be an expert on the ailments of our society, there are those who can. These experts are the very masters who declared our forty fifth President to have the mind of a schoolyard bully. They even wrote a book about it. If you can't trust the word of a proven expert, who then can you trust?

I once wrote a short book called "Naturals." It was about female artists, in the realm of acting. They had, and some continue to have natural ability. They, along with ballplayers, sculptors, paint artists, and countless others, are the exceptions. Most finished school, but had or have an undeniable natural ability that set(s) them apart. I, personally, had a doctor, who was a high school dropout.

Harry Truman was our 33rd President. He was also a high school dropout. While your host certainly doesn't encourage not finishing school, it's best to examine natural ability. President Truman had the ability to lead, and he knew, having served in the Senate from 1934 to 1945, how government worked. He didn't simply walk in and declare himself a candidate for office, out of a thirst for power. An office for which, traditionally, experience is implied, but not required. There's a book, entitled "Strong Men," by Ruth Ben-Ghiat, which, should you need more clarification, your author strongly recommends reading.

Steve Bannon, once the right hand man to the forty fifth President, but has since fallen out of favor, said, for the record, that he'd like to 'burn it all down.' And what? Rebuild it? In your own image, perhaps? Bannon, a sworn Lennonist, is also on the record as a promoter of 'chaos and anarchy' as an American solution. Admittedly, your host was once a proponent of the same chaos and anarchy. The difference is that your host was, at the time, a teenager, and outgrew the concept.

But enough about past Presidents and their henchmen. Let's stay focused on fascism. Turns out, the past President is fascism, so apparently, we'll stay focused on him. He's a difficult man with which to keep up. Every time you think you've got a handle on his shenanigans, he comes up with something new and even more dictatorial in nature. Now he believes that the chairman of the Joint Chiefs, a man he appointed, should be executed for treason, for the high crime of having gone to China in order to insure that they (China) don't start a nuclear war. I, for one, am glad he made the trip. It is his job, no? He's also come right out and said that, if elected, he'll do away with the networks that don't speak favorably about him. Seems like freedom of the Press should fit in here, somewhere. Networks such as NBC, ABC, CNN and MSNBC will be no more, simply for telling the truth. Sounds like a dictatorship to me.

20.

In 1935, it was Sinclair Lewis who declared that "When fascism comes to America, it will be wrapped in the flag and carrying a cross." Let's examine the statement. Fascists are the first to declare their patriotism, even when they, themselves, are bankrupt of that particular loyalty. They are the first to swear their loyalty to the Constitution, but also the first to ban a book. Book banning requires the 'objection' of only one parent. And, given the fact that libraries are included in the ban, they're not very fussy about that parent being an actual parent.

You read it here first: now even you, with no children, can ban a book, tho you'll have to pretend you represent a library. It's real easy. Just get a library card. The one thing that hasn't changed since your author's own childhood is the procurement of a library card. You simply walk in and ask. No questions or proof of identity is required. Just ask, and within minutes you'll have your very own library card, to abuse as you, the card holder, sees fit. Perhaps you'll challenge a book, or maybe its Constitutional right to have a place on the library's book shelf. It now requires the challenge of just one of you.

Now, with regard to the 'carrying a cross' part, while your author makes no claim of Biblical expertise, the fascist does. I only know that the Bible was written by men, not gods. I won't spend a lot of time quoting Biblical passages, as that's not why we're here, but what I will do is to demonstrate how the fascist justifies his or her every move with the declaration that "It's in the Bible!" Never mind that Jesus, one of the Bible's most premiere characters, spoke no English and, if you're to believe it, word for word, had dark skin. Or that he championed only the poor and downtrodden. According to the scripture, he gave his last piece of bread to a starving man. Remember that, next time you reach for the phone, to send money for fattening the pocket of a televangelist.

In a court of law, if the Bible were on trial, arguing for its validity, it would lose almost as famously as our forty fifth President lost in a lawsuit, to a summary judgement. For those unfamiliar with the term, it simply means no trial, and cut to the award. About $450,000,000.

Once upon a time, the Bible was the only law known by the human race. And live by it, they did. Burned a lot of suspected Witches at the stake. If you've ever felt yourself, becoming consumed more and more by fire, then you know it can be quite a painful death. The irony? That none of the 'suspected' witches was an actual crooked-nosed Witch. But they, having been early Americans, needed a bad guy, and the Witch filled the bill. Being female, she usually offered up little or no strength, making her easily arrested. Of course, she could protest her incarceration, usually in a small room with no windows, though it generally fell on deaf ears. After all, she was 'just' a woman. She dared not keep potions, magic or otherwise, as they were certainly a byproduct of Witchcraft. You may have heard of the Salem Witch Trials. Makes for a fascinating read, but don't look for any happy endings.

We've already discussed how the so-called patriot commits an evil deed, then blames the American system of jurisprudence for his or her decline into lawlessness. Now, without getting too technical, let's discuss the law itself. We, here in America, are a nation of laws. While I'm sure you've heard that phrase, probably many times, have you ever given it any real thought? It means that no man or woman is above the law. Not even the President. Well, not while he's in office, anyway. But that's only eight years, tops. It means that any man or any woman can, at any time be prosecuted for having broken the law. So long as they're a civilian, and Presidents, except for four or eight years, always qualify. In most cases, non-citizens also qualify. That said, what's all the fuss? The Supreme Court could upend the 'nation of laws' concept for 45. Given that three members of the Court (out of seven) were appointed by one President, look for that to probably happen.

Patriotism and the Bible are the two sacred cows of American lore. Most of us are fully agreed upon one subject or another. Like the Bible, the Constitution leaves itself open to a myriad of interpretation. In other words, its real meaning can be bent to suit the user's, be they behind a pulpit or in a car, with red lights and siren. Hence, "It's in the Bible!" or "I have my Constitutional rights!" take on a more legitimate meaning. Yes, you have a Constitutional right to fly a flag, laden with only a huge swastika, even though better men than you have died to preserve that right. You even have a Constitutional right to be a Witch.

Our Republic is now under siege by only a handful of zealots, who believe, among other ludicrous principles, only in the word(s) of one person. Shades of Jim Jones? Let's look at the parallels. Jim Jones required that you turn over all your money and property to him. While that 'one person' doesn't yet require that you turn over your money and property, he does ask, repeatedly, for donations. So repeatedly, that it becomes easier to give him $20 than to read the rants of his lieutenant. This, even though the 'one person' claims to be one of the richest men on the planet, whom offered, you may recall in 2016, to foot the bill for ALL his campaigning." Another lie.

No one seems to know what it is that possesses a person to come under the spell of a certifiable lunatic. Jim Jones courted 'directionless' people. Same difference, with significant exceptions. Today's directionless warriors have guns, FOX TV and the internet. Most, with little or no training, are capable of using all three. The internet is a double edged sword. It can be used for good, as I've demonstrated in pages past, or for bad. Only a small number of the Jones warriors had guns, and there was no FOX or internet. But they knew, as history demonstrated, how to use the guns. And when Jones said "jump!" they'd simply ask, "How high?" See any parallels yet?

Jones used religion as a tool to suck in followers, as did Charles Manson. They'd tried every door, you see, and religion was, for most, the final door. That hasn't changed. There is a significant 'religious right', the right that dispatched the group we spoke of, to Uganda, and that continues to have a powerful voice in most American elections. Our forty fifth President makes an occasional reference to 'the good book' – he even sells them to raise money, autographed -- but only when it suits his needs, or in the event of a photo-op. And he'll be sure to hold the Bible, right side up, should that photo-op arrive. Next, if the 'one person' asked you to shoot a stranger dead, in the middle of Fifth Avenue, would you do it? Of course you would. Oh, I'm aware of how he gloated when the prospect of his shooting someone dead on a main street would garner him no repercussions, but this is about you, the dedicated follower, and why you insist on following him. So uh, should he ask you, his follower, to drink deadly poisonous Kool-Aid, because everyone else is drinking it, would you? Of course not. Then you couldn't vote for him.

Another phrase thrown around by the current leader of the Republican Party is "A lot of people say..." or "People tell me..." Who exactly are these people to whom you continually refer? He never quite says who they are. Could it be because these 'people' don't exist, except perhaps in his microscopic mind? He claims the people talk to him "all the time." Hmmm. Do they whisper in his ear, or just blurt it out? Is this the one-time leader of the free world, or someone in desperate need of a straitjacket?

The choice is simple. Either you help us out, promoting peace, prosperity and progress, or you "choose" the side of violence, division and hate. I put the word choose in quotes because I refuse to believe that living in the USA requires the taking of a side. You may say "Violence, division and hate are so much more fun! Never a dull moment!" Having the time of your lives, are you? Sooner or later, the fun ends. You'll have to put away your guns and do the work. Your leader never said it was going to be easy. You're now a foot soldier. You're being led around by the nose. Your leader is a man who's a proven certifiable moron. He's cheated his way through all the finest colleges, and has the 'friends' to prove it.

21.

I spoke briefly about Voters' Rights and gerrymandering in chapters past. Now it's time, in closing, for a bit more depth. First off, if you truly want things to change in your state, vote.I can't say it enough. It's how we get things done or undone. Granted, it seems like it sometimes takes forever, but hang in there, and you'll eventually see a change. Elections in every county are strictly regulated and closely watched. No exceptions. And, as I once conveyed, a school board member or State Senator or Congressman can be elected by as few as one or two votes. Sort of shoots that "My vote doesn't count" theory all to hell, huh?

Also stated elsewhere, the USA is the only country in the world that uses an electoral college for Presidential elections. Some say it's outdated and should be scrapped, an ideology with which your author agrees, by the by, though the Founding Fathers thought it necessary for inclusion. Bare in mind that only property owners were allowed to vote at the time, and there was no such thing as the "Black Vote." Blacks were still slaves, so it wouldn't make much sense, if you were a property and slave owner, to let them vote. They might, after all, have had a ballot measure to, of all things, free themselves.

Barack Obama, the former President, and Eric Holder, the 82nd Attorney General, have spearheaded an organization called the National Democratic Redistricting Committee (NDRC), which attempts to reign in gerrymandering, on a national level. According to its website, the NDRC's accomplishments include "Leveling the playing field with Republicans, on redistricting, by backing litigation, supporting reforms and electing fair-map Democrats." By all accounts, their successes have been moderate.

Anti-gerrymandering efforts were, however, successful in Alabama. They can only be successful if you, the voter, get out or stay in, and vote. How does one stay in and vote? By voting absentee. However, there's a caveat that your author feels compelled to include. When voting absentee, if possible, take your completed ballot to the registrar of voters. Every county has one. Remember? Most absentee ballots require a signature, usually on the outside of the envelope. If so, Sign it only in the presence of a clerk. Seems like a lot of work just to cast a vote, but, as is usually the case, you'll only have to do it twice a year, and if your vote is sure to be counted, you'll follow the above simple instructions.

I wouldn't trust the 'drop boxes' that are placed in plain sight, on streets or street corners. Especially those with armed guards. At the risk of instilling paranoia, which I certainly don't mean to do, there's just too much that can happen to a ballot, between where it's picked up, and its final destination.

If you wait until voting day, which most Americans do, here are a few simple rules by which you can safely cast your ballot:

Bring plenty of water. Some states, purely out of meanness, have made it illegal to give water to a person standing in line, waiting to vote, regardless of the weather. Food, depending on the length of the line, is optional.

While waiting on line, mind your business, stay quiet and look straight ahead. There may be those who'd believe they can influence your vote, by harassment, intimidation or other means. You could also be arrested, should you choose to not stay quiet.

Whenever possible, arrange to vote in groups of four or more. Some states have made this illegal, however, there's security in numbers, and it'll give you someone to talk to, while waiting on line.

Don't be scared. In polling places, uniformed police officers are the only people authorized to carry guns in plain sight. Even the 'open carry' states. Voting is the sacred right of every American over the age of eighteen. It's what insures us a Democracy. This includes polling places.

If you must speak, be courteous. Don't give them a reason to have you arrested, and subsequently, no vote is cast on your behalf. If you're a Democrat, you should assume that they're looking for one of those reasons.

A good rule by which to live, when in a polling place, is to speak only when spoken to. While the phrase may be grammatically incorrect, I'm sure you, the reader, will get the point. Don't speak about the election in which you're about to vote.

States with a predominantly Republican Senate or House will invariably make it more difficult for people to vote. It's usually the Southern states. While your author promised not to make this a political rant, facts are facts, and when people are given the unencumbered freedom to vote, Democrats tend to get elected. Politicians resort to fascism in order to obtain their goals. Fascism is here, dressed in a suit and tie, and it's not going away any time soon. Rachel Maddow's book, "PREQUEL An American Fight Against Fascism" is on sale now, and this author suggests a reading of said book. The treatise deals on a more in-depth level, with American fascism and its origins, which go back about eighty years. It names names, which I've mostly avoided doing, for reasons, legal and otherwise.

There are two kinds of fascists. One is political in nature. Remember that guy who promised to give you everything, in return for your vote? And one is the fascist citizen, who likes his toys. Toys including, but not limited to AR15's and AK47's. One is disguised, as mentioned, in suit and tie. One dresses in street clothes and has an unusually low IQ, probably not contoured to the level of the politician. He/she reports for work every day, at a no-future job, they probably hate. But when the weekend gets here, time to get out the toys – the truck, the guns and the action movie – and have some fun.

Perhaps you'll justify the use of guns, either by their numbers alone – over forty million in the USA -- the severity of the enemy, or to "keep the peace," as in law enforcement. That said, I've seen the destruction and loss of life that can be accomplished with only one shot, and I can not justify their use. A policeman or woman, with a gun strapped to their body, will most certainly agree. Remember, the average cop, during his/her career, never fires a weapon.

Peaceful co-existence is not a new concept. It's been around since the dawn of the human race. More recently, it was in a song, penned by John Lennon, and called "Imagine." Fifty or so years ago, it was a concept chuckled off and so shrouded in drug use that very few, including its proponents, took it seriously. You may remember the hippies. They were onto a good thing, and most didn't even know it. There were those of us who took peaceful coexistence seriously, though by and large, it was laughed off by a generation that claimed to wake up, take a shower, get a haircut, and set out to enjoy a small piece of the American or European Dream.

The core belief persisted. The belief, by many that the human race can and will coexist, regardless of the pigment in our skin; regardless of how we may speak a language other than English; regardless of the religion to which we align ourselves. With the myriad of issues that make us different to look at or listen to, we can at least agree on one thing: We all bleed red. A well placed bullet can and will bring an immediate end to this thing we know as our lifetime.

I've kept 'Ban This Book' purposely short because, with the advent of the internet, people tend to get their information elsewhere, and then skim the information, at best. Granted, I've only given you, the reader, one side of the fascism story. To give you another perspective, there are numerous books and movies I've recommended. As for the 'other side,' of the story of fascism, not sure there is another side, but seek out books to read, being certain they're not conspiratorial in nature. Should you find one, it's probably an unquestionable non-truth.

ACKNOWLEDGEMENTS

THINK IMPACT

EDVISORS NETWORK Both for available scholarships and college tuitions.

NATIONAL COALITION AGAINST CENSORSHIP

Nicole Hockley, Mark Barden, Bill Sherlack of the **SANDYHOOK PROMISE**

David Hogg of NEVER AGAIN, MARCH FOR OUR LIVES and **LEADERS WE DESERVE**

Rachel Maddow for podcast of **ULTRA** and her book, "Prequel"

CONSTITUTION and DECLARATION OF INDEPENDENCE courtesy of **CITIZENSHIP AND IMMIGRATION SERVICES**

STACEY ZEZZA, Library Media Technician at EAST AVENUE SCHOOL in Hayward, CA

BARBARA BEUYS and **FRANK MCDONOUGH with contributions from TANJA B. SPITZER** for "Sophie Scholl: A Biography"

HAYWARD HISTORICAL SOCIETY Hayward, CA

PENAmerica New York Headquarters (pen.org) for various chapters regarding book banning in America.

Deborah Reade for Stop Forever WIPP foundation

Grace Slick

Iris DeMent

Britannica

Sun Tzu

Pleasantville (film)

Collossus: The Forbin Projectgoto (film)

Coca-Cola

"Strong Men" by Ruth Ben Ghiat

Icangotocollege.com ALBERT EINSTEIN;

ALBERT EINSTEIN;

COLOSSUS: THE FORBIN PROJECT;

ROBERT FULGHUM for ALL I NEED TO KNOW I LEARNED IN KINDERGARTEN;

JOHN LENNON for IMAGINE

www.ingramcontent.com/pod-product-compliance
Lightning Source LLC
Chambersburg PA
CBHW050443150626
46551CB00028B/1171